They Went

To Carry the Gospel to the World

By

Ken Sewell, Ph.D.

SUNSET
INSTITUTE PRESS
3728 34th Street • Lubbock, Texas • 79410
1 (800) 687-2121 • Email: extschool@sibi.cc

"They Went"

Copyright © 2004
Sunset Institute Press

Printed and Bound in the
United States of America
All Rights Reserved

Cover Design by Beth E. Miller

ISBN 0-9755183-8-0 (pbk.)

Reviewers' Comments

As much as possible, Ken Sewell has allowed the fingerprints of each missionary to remain on his own story. New missionaries will be guided by this book. Veteran missionaries will thrill to hear and compare their stories with those of fellow adventurers in the world's mission fields. Elderships and mission committees will be drawn to these stories as men are drawn to light in a dark world.

– Robert K. Oglesby, Sr.
Pulpit Minister
Waterview Church of Christ

Ken Sewell has captured the essence of the motivations which can successfully see a missionary through the trials and struggles of cross cultural communications and church planting. This book is a "must read" for church missions committees, current and future missionaries and for those who are training missionaries. Missions methodology is taught subtly and practically through the real-life stories of those who took the great commission to heart. Truly, "they went."

– Truitt Adair
Executive Director
Sunset International Bible Institute

Dedication

This book is dedicated to all of the magnificent men and women who have traveled the globe or gone next door to take the gospel message to a lost and dying world.

Acknowledgments

The author is profoundly grateful to the fourteen wonderful people who graciously consented to having their interviews included in this book. All are dedicated servants of our Lord. In alphabetical order they are:

Kevin Carson
Jeff Hatcher
Gary Jackson
Jody Jones
Bill and Owana Kidd
Michael Landon
Chris Nichol

Tim Pyles
Glenn and Glenda Rodgers
Patrick Sheaffer
Roger Thompson
and Dwight Whitsett

The author is also thankful for the encouragement and kind words of the following people:

Truitt Adair
Herman Alexander
Howard Norton
Robert K. Oglesby, Sr.

Special thanks go to Robert K. Oglesby, Sr. for writing the Preface.

The Sunset Institute Press has been a delight to work with and has contributed immeasurably to this book.

Without the encouragement, proofreading, and suggestions of my wife Eudena, this book would be only a thought in my heart. She is the wind behind my sails.

The author has donated all proceeds from the sale of this book to Sunset International Bible Institute in recognition of their tremendous influence on training evangelists to take the gospel message to people lost in sin. My thanks go to all of the dedicated SIBI staff and the Sunset elders for their valuable efforts to take the gospel throughout the world.

The author will appreciate receiving comments at ken_sewell@yahoo.com.

v

Preface

The New Testament offers us some examples and some principles of mission work, particularly that of the Apostle Paul. Much of what we read there we find difficult to transplant into our modern world. How does the church learn how to do mission work?

Dr. Ken Sewell has approached foreign missions from a different perspective than the one professional missiologists normally use. This book is not about numbers, statistics, bar graphs, culture patterns, or any broad sweeping rules.

To help us understand foreign mission work, Ken has cashed in his 40 years of serving on mission committees. His method has been to simply interview returned missionaries and let them tell their stories with little or no commentary from him. As much as possible, he has allowed the fingerprints of each missionary to remain on his own story.

Their stories come back to us from all over the world in such far-flung places as North America, South America, Central America, Europe, Africa, and Australia. The stories are as varied as the geography and the personalities involved. The mission plans had variety, and the results were like the world we live in; that is, a mixture of success and failure. Always, however, there were lessons learned.

In this book those stories have been told and the lessons have been captured oftentimes in the mission worker's own words. Actually, this is a book about learning from one's experience. Once the formal mission education and the home country are left behind, the real learning begins. Language, culture, and new experiences shape the missionary like sand peeling the rough surface from a rock. When the experience is over, a wiser missionary emerges.

Unlike some academic writers, Ken has been on many short terms excursions to the mission field. He has learned enough to know that it is best to allow the missionaries to speak for themselves rather than offering expert opinions.

However, in his last chapter, Ken favors us with some common lessons that it seems all missionaries learn no matter where they serve the Lord.

New missionaries will be guided by this book. Veteran missionaries will thrill to hear and compare their stories with those of fellow adventurers in the world's mission fields. Elderships and mission committees will be drawn to these stories as men are drawn to light in a dark world.

Robert K. Oglesby, Sr.
Pulpit Minister
Waterview Church of Christ
Richardson, Texas

Table of Contents

Chapter One

Missions and Mission Teams

*B*efore he ascended to the right hand of God, Jesus told his disciples, *"This is what is written: The Christ will suffer and rise from the dead on the third day, and repentance and forgiveness of sins will be preached in his name to all nations, beginning at Jerusalem. You are witnesses of these things. I am going to send you what my Father has promised; but stay in the city until you have been clothed with power from on high . . . . All authority in heaven and on earth has been given to me. Therefore go and make disciples of all nations, baptizing them in the name of the Father and of the Son and of the Holy Spirit, and teaching them to obey everything I have commanded you...* *Go into all the world and preach the good news to all creation. Whoever believes and is baptized will be saved, but whoever does not believe will be condemned. And surely I am with you always, to the very end of the age."* (A compilation of Luke 24:46-49, Matthew 28:18-19, and Mark 16:15,16 NIV.)

The apostles obeyed Jesus and went, witnessing about seeing the Lord in the flesh, seeing him die, seeing him after he was resurrected, and seeing him ascend into the sky with a promise of coming again. They began witnessing on Pentecost about ten days after Jesus ascended into heaven and continued until their death. Even when they were opposed, beaten, or threatened, they continued. Acts 5:47 NIV tells us that, *"Day after day, in the temple courts and from house to house, they never stopped teaching and proclaiming the good news that Jesus is the Christ."* Just as

Jesus said, they were his witnesses in Jerusalem, and in all Judea and Samaria, and to the ends of the earth (Acts 1:8). Paul said, late in his life, *"You know that I have not hesitated to preach anything that would be helpful to you but have taught you publicly and from house to house. I have declared to both Jews and Greeks that they must turn to God in repentance and have faith in our Lord Jesus."* (Acts 20:20 NIV)

Jesus laid a task on His disciples that must be repeated generation after generation. We haven't seen Jesus in the flesh, but we have the eyewitnesses' accounts in the New Testament. And we have the faith those eyewitness accounts have built in our hearts. It is our task to relay the apostles' witnessing to all creation, i.e. every creature. As Danny Miller recently quoted Roy Deaver from the Gospel Advocate,

> "Think what is involved in the phrase, 'To every creature.' If the Lord had said, 'Preach the gospel in every continent,' this would have been a task. But the Lord said far more. If the Lord had said, 'Preach the gospel in every nation,' this would have been a greater task. But, the Lord said far more. If the Lord had said, 'Preach the gospel in every city' the task would have been far greater. But the Lord said more. If the Lord had said, 'Preach the gospel in every house,' the burden would have been tremendous, but the Lord said even more. The gospel of Christ must be preached to 'Every person in every house on every street, lane, road, and trail, of every city, village, and district, of every nation of the whole world.'" (*The Correspondent*, Winter 2003, published by Sunset International Bible Institute, Lubbock, Texas).

God be praised. There are still men and women who are obeying Jesus' command to go into the entire world and share the good news. This book presents vignettes of twelve such families who went. The vignettes are based on personal interviews with individuals who have preached and taught in the mission field. Some have returned from the mission field, yet every one is still involved in missions, either by renewing their own spirits before returning, training those who will go, or in short-term missions. All of the twelve families feel the need to share the gospel with the world. And, although each knows he or she cannot tell everyone about Christ, they are telling those they meet. That's the way Jesus intended the world to learn about Him.

Not only is there a need for people to go and share the good news, there is a desperate need for people who will send them. We often think the mission team is the group of people going to teach in the same city. But, the mission team is larger than that. It includes those who give from their physical wealth so others may share the spiritual wealth. In Romans 10:14,15, the writer describes the team.

> *"Everyone who calls on the name of the Lord will be saved. How, then, can they call on the one they have not believed in? And how can they believe in the one of whom they have not heard? And how can they hear without someone **preaching** to them? And how can they preach unless they are **sent**? As it is written, how beautiful are the feet of those **who bring good news!**"*

The folks who stay home, earn income, and give of their income to assist the ones who go are a critical and necessary part of the mission team. Don't think missionaries don't appreciate the folks sending the money. They do, just as Paul appreciated the Philippians for sending time and time again to meet his needs.

A critical part of the sending team is the elders of the overseeing congregation. They have a responsibility to make sure the missionaries receive appropriate care and support: physically, mentally, and spiritually. Elders must also realize that returning missionaries have needs as they reenter their home culture. As you will see, adapting to the old culture is harder and more stressful than moving into the new, foreign culture. What has been termed culture shock is real and can be devastating if not properly dealt with. Reverse culture shock can be just as overwhelming.

It is the author's hope and prayer, that this book will, in a small way, assist both parts of the mission team: the senders and the goers. Prospective missionaries should be able to get a bit of a feel for what they will experience in the field. They can see that their experiences will take them to spiritual mountaintops, but they may also plunge them into emotional depths. Paul told Christians to take up the whole spiritual armor because he knew the devil would never quit trying to thwart their work. Knowledge of what God's servants may encounter can form a part of that shield of faith necessary to quench the evil one's flaming arrows. The arrows will come, and usually when the work seems to be going best. The worker must be prepared. God is always there and much more powerful than the evil one.

Active missionaries may gather ideas from other people's approaches to sharing the good news. It has often been said that there is no right way to do mission work. Whatever methods are effective, as long as they are scriptural, are good methods. Sometimes, methods need to change as conditions change.

Missionaries can gather strength from knowing that other missionaries are experiencing many of the same things they are, although they work many miles away and in an entirely different culture.

Hopefully, the senders, those who oversee and support, will gain a better understanding of what the people on the front line are experiencing. Leaving one's home culture and going to a strange new environment is both an adventure and a trial. Interestingly, none of the people I have interviewed would trade their experiences for a comfortable life. They delight at seeing awareness brighten the student's eyes as they learn about Jesus. They feast on helping the new converts grow into healthy spiritual adults. They endure the hard times so they can revel in people's happiness in serving Christ and leaving sin behind. Let's share in their joy and tribulations as we read their stories and meditate on the truths therein.

Each story is based upon an interview with a missionary. In each case, I have tried to be transparent and relay the person's story in as close to his or her own words as I could. It's only right, as the stories are theirs. In one case, the missionary wrote his own chapter. I hope these vignettes inspire you as much as they have me during the interviews and subsequent writing. Missionaries are special people. Thank God for men and women who will go taking the good news with them, and thank God for those who send.

Wouldn't it be wonderful if God would say about each of us what he said about David? *"I have found David son of Jesse a man after my own heart; he will do everything I want him to do."* (Acts 13:23 NIV) Are we doing everything God wants us to do to reach the lost?

As you read the stories of men and women who have taken the gospel message to the world, consider the items that are common and those that are different. Consider the obstacles and consider their victories. Feel the passion that stirred these individuals to go into the world.

Chapter Two

Mexico

Based on an interview with Jody Jones

*M*exico? "No way," the team decided. Five couples studying at Sunset International Bible Institute were searching the world for the right spot to plant the church. They had committed to go; the question was, "Where?"

Gerald Paden suggested they spend their spring break week at a house in Mexico where they could pray and meditate as they sought God's guidance. While there, the team decided to visit Toluca's market, the largest in Mexico. Toluca has a population of over 300,000 and lies forty miles west of Mexico City. Not appreciating what Holy Week means in a Catholic country, they selected Good Friday as the day to visit the market. When they arrived, the city's beauty, sparse traffic, and lack of trash impressed them. They decided they could live and work in this lovely city set close to the lushly green-draped Nevado de Toluca volcano. No church of Christ existed in the city, and they felt the lostness of many souls. They believed this was the place God wanted them. A few of the team had been too sick to make the trip, but they eagerly accepted the other's recommendation. That evening the team prayed and committed to take the pure gospel message to Toluca.

Later, Jody and a team member who had missed the first trip to Toluca because of sickness made a survey trip in preparation for their move. It wasn't Good Friday, and everything except the volcano had changed; the traffic and trash had returned with a vengeance. The team member asked Jody what they had seen in this city. Jody could only say, "It didn't looked like this when we were here." But, the team had committed, and in spite of this new depressing image of the city, they pressed on. They were convinced that this was where God wanted them to preach.

Before moving, they completed school and raised support. Rather than each couple seeking to raise their own support, they approached this task as a team. Supporters committed to the work rather than an individual. Each couple secured a sponsoring congregation, and the team visited several churches seeking funds. Jody reported to at least eleven congregations throughout their eleven-year-plus effort.

Money raised, three couples moved to Toluca in January 1991. Another family came eight months later and another in January 1992 after they graduated from Sunset International Bible Institute. The team consisted of best friends Jody and Raeanne Jones, Jack and Clare Dyas, Barry and Denise Galindo, Curt and Jenny Peter, and Rodger and Dena Henderson. This would be the Jones' home for eleven years and three months. The Dyas worked there for nine years, and the Galindos for ten. The Peters and Hendersons returned to the U.S earlier due to medical and family problems. The entire team still considers themselves best friends.

Why did the Jones family decide to enter the mission field? They heard missionaries' reports about large numbers of people seeking God while there just weren't enough teachers. Their hearts were touched. They had already experienced difficulty in interesting fellow Texans to study God's word. With hearts yearning to teach lost souls and knowing that God loves all people everywhere, they committed to plant a church and stay until the job was done.

In preparing to go, they learned that the average tenure of church of Christ missionaries was only eighteen months. "That's too short a time to develop the leaders necessary to sustain a healthy church," Jody said. "Planting a church and leaving too soon is like having a baby and abandoning it on a deserted hillside." The Joneses promised each other that they would stay until the church could sustain itself. In their minds, sustaining itself included both financial strength and scriptural leadership.

With their two children aged eight and five, they moved into this strange new culture in January 1991. They didn't know the language so they enrolled in language schools. The team had planned to spend the first year learning the language and the culture before formally beginning the work. "The schools helped, but I really learned the language during bible classes," Jody said.

During the first few months, the team met in their houses. They handed out literature in the streets and attracted a few students. Two students put on their Lord in baptism that first year. After six months, they held their first worship in Spanish and Jody said their Spanish was awful. All of them continued to develop their language skills, and after bilingual Barry Galindo arrived in January 1992, worship was always in Spanish.

Although they studied culture shock before moving, and identified it when it began to rear its ugly head, they couldn't avoid it. It began to overwhelm them. Jody said, "I reacted to the shock by not studying the Word or praying as I had been doing. When I began to study more and pray more intently, I came out of it. Focusing on God and His mission was critical to my well-being."

The work began to blossom during the second year after they rented a meeting place. Knowing the language, they could talk with people on their heart-level. People began to respond and twenty-six became Christ's disciples that year. After two years, Sunday morning attendance grew to about seventy-five and they moved to a larger meeting hall. In the next two years, the attendance grew to about one hundred thirty.

The Mexican people networked with their friends, family, and neighbors. Literature handouts were no longer needed. The Mexicans were eager to learn although their Catholic heritage taught they couldn't understand God's word. Yet, they found that when they read the Bible, they could understand it. Then, they wanted their networking group to experience the same joy. Thus, there were always plenty of people ready to study.

"Days in the Country" became a major attraction for newcomers and members. On the first Sunday of the month after worship, they loaded their vans with people and food and headed for a park on the outskirts of the city. Everyone enjoyed the potluck meals and sports such as volleyball, baseball, and other games. The urban dwellers really enjoyed the chance to get out of the congested city and embraced this day of fun and fellowship. The first Sunday of the month had the highest attendance as members invited friends and family members to enjoy the day.

Jody believes that immediately establishing a Bible Institute and opening it for all was the single most important thing they did. Two nights a week, they taught courses similar to those taught by their Alma Mata, Sunset International Bible Institute. Sometimes, the Bible Institute hosted classes four nights per week. From the Bible Institute's students came the elders, deacons, evangelists, and teachers that now serve this ongoing congregation. Following SIBI's practice, the Bible Institute granted two levels of certificates to those completing the curriculum. The team also taught fundamental classes on Sunday morning and gave certificates to those who completed the courses. Jody said, "I would compare the Mexican students with any in the U.S. schools. They wanted to learn and dove into the material with joy and perseverance."

Team relationships are critical to sharing the good news and living a life that illustrates the teachers believe the message they are sharing. This team met every week to communicate problems and successes and to discuss visions and goals. Jody said the most important part of the meeting was the hour they spent in intensive prayer together. They all prayed individually, but in combining their prayers, they felt the presence of God and His graciousness. They had three columns on their prayer list; the seeking lost, the members, and personal needs. Watching people's names move from the lost to the member's column encouraged them.

The team is convinced that these periods of intensive prayer caused the average number of baptisms to grow to sixty per year for the last three years they were there. Jody gave God the credit and emphasized that seventy were baptized the year after they left.

The team concentrated on using everyone's strengths and did not try to force each one into a common mold. They recognized that each person possessed individual talents and encouraged each one to strengthen his or her skills. The men met for breakfast once per week and used the time to hold each other accountable for his goals. Early in the work, they determined to decide issues by consensus rather than elections, as they were concerned that in elections some won and others lost.

Before they would meet with the congregation to discuss an issue, the missionaries would thrash it out and come to a consensus. When the issue was brought before the congregation, the team would present a unified front. This helped the congregation realize that they could compromise just as the missionaries did and adapt to each other's feeling and ideas. The locals knew the missionaries did not always agree, and bent their own desires for the common good because of their respect for each other. They witnessed how the missionaries resolved conflict and supported the group consensus and goals. The team remains best friends to this day.

From the beginning, the team focused on training the new Christians to assume full responsibility for the congregation. Whenever possible, a local Christian baptized the new convert. Then, they encouraged each new Christian to enroll in the Bible Institute and to bring his or her friends and family to bible studies.

During his tenure, Jody and his family returned about once a year to report to their sponsoring and supporting congregations. They found living from a suitcase for a month to be stressful. During the visit, they would report to each of the eleven congregations providing financial support. Often, they had no vacation.

There were many discouraging events during their work in Toluca. Jody lost his father's parents, his mother's mother, and a great-grandmother while in Mexico. All were dear Christian people he misses tremendously. In addition, they had to move into a gated community when kidnappers targeted his children. Their family had increased to six with the births of two children in Toluca, one in 1993 and one in 1995. They endured robberies, loss of some support from home, accusations of false teaching from supporters, and other of Satan's wiles.

Several youth and adult groups from Texas visited Toluca to perform service projects. Evangelistic campaigns were not encouraged for fear the Tolucans might consider seeking the lost to be a big annual event instead of their every day responsibility. The team organized a Toluca Workshop every two years and invited all of their supporters. About forty supporters came to each event. Visits from the north-of-the-border Christians encouraged both the team and the Tolucans. Those who came always left excited and edified.

Jody offers any prospective missionary the following advice:

Make sure God calls you to the work. Pray about it, and when doors open step though.

Set goals for mission work and do not leave until the goals are attained. The biggest problem in mission work is that the work is abandoned too soon. Remember the example of Hernán Cortés. Before he started his campaign to conquer the Aztecs, he burned his ships and told his followers they must conquer or die. Cortés was committed to the task. Similarly, missionaries must be prepared to stay 8 to 12 years if planting a new church.

Be prepared to endure discouragement. Missionaries face many disheartening times with sickness, physical danger, robberies, loss of support from home, discouragement from family, and on and on.

Have a sense of mission for God. You will need it to continue through the hard times.

Be an equipper, not just an evangelist. You must turn over responsibility to locals as soon as possible. One way to begin is to get someone to manage local funds, and then turn more and more responsibility to members as they become able to handle it. Always search for responsibilities to share.

Learn the language, as it is impossible to get to the heart level through translators. Learn as much language as possible before going, even if you get the wrong dialect and pronunciation. Any little bit helps.

Be real with natives; show your vulnerability and needs to them. Mexicans usually deal with each other on a superficial level. By being open, the team formed the deep relationships necessary for real growth.

Be sure you leave enough time for family, take a day off each and every week. Their team held each other accountable for taking family time. Everyone took Mondays off, and was confident that this helped them stay in the field.

Jody returned to Texas because he felt the church in Mexico no longer needed him. He stated that if he stayed, the Tolucans would have continued to look to him for leadership instead of their elders. Jody saw his role similar to that of John the Baptist, to diminish so that the church could become greater. When he left, the church had elders, deacons, several bible teachers, and a native evangelist. They supported themselves financially and continued to reach out. As stated earlier, they converted seventy souls the year after the team left.

However, the Toluca church experienced a rough first year after the Jones left. Not heeding the team's warning, the elders held closed meeting and shut out the other leaders in the church. Dissention ensued since members felt disenfranchised. Fortunately, that is behind them now, and the church continues to grow.

When the Jones family returned to Texas, they found that reverse culture shock was worse than the culture shock of moving to Mexico. Many things had changed and Texas society's march toward materialism was evident. Abundance was everywhere, in the grocery stores, in the malls, on the roads, and in houses. Movies and television programs promoted a materialistic and worldly spirit. They missed their Mexican friends. They found they had forgotten how to do simple things required to sustain life here, such as handling utilities and groceries. The number of options they had to consider in getting a telephone was mind numbing.

The worse thing in the reverse culture shock was what they perceived as a cold and distant reception by their Christian brothers and sisters. In Mexico, it was a terrifically big occasion to meet a Christian. In Texas, it was no big deal, and often, the new acquaintance looked upon them with suspicion.

Jody said he considered going to another mission field when they left Mexico, but wasn't sure he was up to it at the time. He thought he could use the same strategies in Texas as he used in Toluca. A church in Athens, TX agreed, and he began a church planting activity in Frisco, TX. At first, it was only the Jones family, but then others aligned themselves and they began to meet in homes. As the congregation grew, other homes were used until the size dictated they move to larger rented facilities. They have now outgrown those facilities and are having difficulty in finding a suitable place to meet. Land costs exceed $70,000 per acre and the school facilities are full with over a two-year waiting list. Jody is confident that God will provide and they continue to seek souls while searching for a larger assembly place.

Thought Provokers
1. How long should teams planting new churches commit for?
2. Do all team members have to commit for the entire term?

3. List three good ways to penetrate a society for Christ?
4. What events dictate when the church planting team should leave?

Chapter Three

Guadalajara

Based upon an interview with Patrick Sheaffer

*W*hile growing up in Yukon, Oklahoma in a Christian family, Patrick fell in love with mission work. At the age of twenty, he enrolled in the Adventures in Missions (AIM) program at Sunset Church of Christ in Lubbock, Texas. By enrolling, he committed to eight months of intense bible and mission study to be followed by eighteen months of service alongside an experienced missionary in some foreign country. After completing the classroom studies, he went to Lisbon, Portugal, and instead of the usual service time, he stayed for thirty-six months. Lengthening his commitment turned out to be a fortunate decision as Malissa Patterson went there during that time for her AIM service.

When they returned, Patrick enrolled in Sunset International Bible Institute (SIBI) and later received a degree from Lubbock Christian University. During this time, he continued to work with the AIM program. He and Melissa formed the most important team in their life when they married. They both wanted to finish SIBI and head back to the mission field.

As part of their work with AIM, they assisted Jay Jarboe each year in taking students to Mexico for an introduction to the mission field. For many students, this was their first opportunity to experience a foreign culture. On one trip in 1994, Chadd and Nancy Schroeder, who were serving as missionaries, shoulder tapped them and asked if they would consider joining them on a mission team. The Schroeders were also ex-AIMers and in love with Mexican people and mission work. The Sheaffers agreed to think about it.

The mission field kept tugging on them, so in 1996 they formed a team with four other SIBI students. The team committed to go, but didn't have a destination. Then, the Schroeders came to Lubbock to study advanced missions. They joined the team and soon they all set their sights on Guadalajara, Mexico. It seemed a natural selection as seventy five percent of the team spoke Spanish and the Sheaffers spoke a related language, Portuguese. Guadalajara had been designated a gateway city as it is Mexico's second largest city with a population of over 1.5 million people. It is also the capitol of the State of Jalisco and is located on the highway between Mexico City and the northern west coast Mexican cities.

Guadalajara is an ancient city by American standards. Founded in 1530, it moved twice before being established at its present location in 1542. The city is a center for magnificent architecture, and its ceramics and pottery are highly prized throughout the world. Since it is located near some of Mexico's most spectacular natural sites, including Puerto Vallarta and the deep green rolling hills of the surrounding parklands, tourists flock to it.

At that time, there were five churches in Guadalajara with a total membership of less than two hundred. The team made several trips to share their vision and received a warm reception. After completing their preparation work, four families moved there in January 1998. The Sheaffers followed in early March with their two month old son.

All team members were ex-AIMers although none were married at the time they were in the AIM program. All the men graduated from SIBI and had at least one degree from a university. SIBI had fueled their desire to carry the gospel to those who had not heard it. The team had diverse backgrounds coming from Texas, Oklahoma, New Mexico, Washington, South Carolina, and Mexico. The native-born Americans were Patrick and Melissa Sheaffer, Jason and Beth Gossett, Joe and Elaine Pruitt, and Shelly Herrera. Robert Herrera was born in Mexico, and crossed the Rio

Grande on the back of his uncle. He became a naturalized citizen before going to SIBI and later marrying Shelly.

The team spent a year in preparation and planning before moving to Guadalajara. Using a chalkboard, they discussed and rehashed what others found worked and what didn't. They envisioned planting a cell based church and developed a three-phased, five-year plan, which detailed responsibilities for each family based upon their skills and personalities.

They envisioned planting multiple congregations that would (1) reflect the Kingdom of God in Guadalajara, (2) have trained and responsible Mexican leadership, and (3) be capable of and committed to reproduction. This first effort would lay the groundwork for a larger church planting movement that would spread across Mexico.

Phase one covered the first year and primarily focused on getting each team family healthy and adapted to the culture so they would be positioned for future growth. They designed the second phase to lay a foundation of growth and reproduction emphasizing evangelism, the development and expansion of a leadership base through a network of small groups, and the development of the essential elements of a healthy and evangelistic congregation. Phase three would cover years six through ten and cover additional growth, transition from a missionary-led church to one led by Mexican leadership, and planting of new congregations.

Each year, they reset the plan, spending time examining how the work had progressed, where they were at that time, and where they needed to go. Patrick says they soon learned the adage, "You plan, God directs." The Guadalajarians weren't receptive to all of their approaches. They tried a variety of methods, including printing and distributing literature, going door to door, preaching in the streets, holding tent meeting, and forming special interest groups. It was a rude awakening. They didn't understand how a highly trained, highly motivated group of young people could not more dramatically impact the city. They had planned on building a big congregation in two years. However, they found the soil rocky in this extremely affluent city.

Although the church didn't develop as rapidly as they had hoped, people were coming to the Lord. In 1999, they began with one cell group of about ten people. By 2001, they had eight cell groups with an average attendance of 56. By 2002, average attendance was 74 and contributions were almost tripled from 1999. Six were baptized in 1999, six in 2000, and twelve more in 2001.

Guadalajara's affluence makes the field rocky. A BMW dealership, a Harley-Davidson store, and a Planet Hollywood restaurant were on the same street as the church. People are materialistic and busy. But once the people put on their Lord, they understood Luke 14 and took up their cross and denied themselves. Many found themselves hated by father, mother, sister, and brother; however, about 90 percent of the converts are still faithful.

The team called on outside resources to assist the work. In the summer of 2000, a Let's Start Talking campaign produced 71 studies, 8 continuing students and 1 baptism. A group from the Comanche Trail church conducted a VBS with 28 children attending, and distributed over 8,000 flyers and invitations. The Sunset Church of Christ conducted a second VBS and over 30 children attended. The group distributed over 16,000 flyers and three precious souls from one family put on their Lord in baptism as a result.

The next summer another Let's Start Talking group came and held 60 studies and baptized three. Four other groups came and held a Friends Camp, distributed literature, and held puppet shows. Attendance increased.

Eleven church members who had stopped attending worship at the existing churches were restored in the first two years and eight placed membership. By the end of 2001, 74 Mexicans, on the average, attended Sunday worship and a record attendance of 124 was established. The La Estancia Church, as it had become known, rented a building to accommodate the Sunday crowds. Patrick says the decision to rent a large facility skewed them away from a cell-based church to a church that had small groups. They have since stopped renting the space and returned to maintaining an office and worshiping at a hotel. All their body-life functions, including training and classes are now conducted in small groups. The congregation continues to grow and, as a growing congregation should, wrestle with the associated problems. The congregation has identified three men as candidates for elders.

After they had been in country for five years, the team began to hear about a new paradigm to maintain the health of long-term missionaries. They had heard about people going to Africa for 30 years without coming home more than twice. Now many experienced missionaries were promoting the idea that missionaries should come out of their work after five or six years to promote both their health and the health of work. They should have an extended furlough time for renewing their spirits, reequipping their approaches, and retooling their skills. One family left after four years and is now in South Carolina planning to return to plant a new church. When Joe Pruitt's mother contracted cancer, the Pruitts went to be with her for about a year. During their absence, several Mexicans stepped up and grew in spirit and service. This confirmed the extended furlough paradigm to the team. Joe and Elaine returned to Guadalajara, determined to spend another six years maturing the present congregation and launching another.

The Sheaffers began asking the Lord what he wanted after they had been there for five years. Should they go through what Patrick called the "recycle mode?" Should they form another team and return to Guadalajara or go somewhere else. They were also being encouraged to return to Lubbock and work with AIM. They weren't completely sure what God wanted for their lives, but recognized that Patrick had a talent for working with AIM students and felt the criticalness of training lifetime missionaries. They returned to AIM in February 2003.

Chadd Schroeder, whom Patrick describes as a visionary, incredible preacher, and developer of their team, recently arrived in Lubbock. The Schroeders spent most of the last 10 years in Mexico where their twin daughters were born. They returned to Lubbock for a year of renewing and plan to go back after recruiting a family to go with them.

The departure of several of the team members has produced some significant transitions since the Sheaffers left. Currently, Sunday attendance averages about 80 to 90 and sometimes reaches100. They have two full time missionary families and one full time paid Mexican evangelist. The six functional small groups network effectively. The AIM tradition continues for the team with the arrival of Tim and Kim Rush. Tim and Kim envision partnering with the other long-time missionary family and the Mexican evangelist for five to seven years.

When asked what he would do differently if starting over, Patrick recalled an article written by Howard Norton several years ago, possibly in the Christian Chronicle. The title of the article was, *What I Wished I Knew When I was in my Thirties.* Patrick kept it taped to his computer in Mexico until it disappeared. Howard Norton had listed eight or so things he would do better such as save money, pray more, and take more time being a church and less time doing church. Patrick gave the following list in the same spirit.

Spend less time talking about how to do mission work and spend more time doing it. He noted that explosive growth came when the team was on their knees in desperate prayer, "Lord we don't know what to do, Do something here." That's when God made thing happen. He wishes they had spent an equal amount of time praying as they did in discussing strategy and work. At first, their meetings would last three hours, and end in prayer. Last year, they flipped it around and began to tell God what they wanted to talk about. When they prayed for an hour and discussed work for an hour, the growth exploded.

Provide the wives more support. They had some people come down to help in this regard. The men needed more awareness of how to care for their family in a healthy nurturing way. Male missionaries must make sure their families are spiritually healthy and not neglected.

Continually update each team member's role. It can be damaging to pigeonhole people in terms of their giftedness. Patrick is gregarious, outgoing, and loves to meet people. Using a popular profiling technique, he fell into the role of encouraging, teaching, and leading in worship, as well as organizing and teaching new members. Looking back, he wishes he had done more personal evangelism. He thinks he didn't see himself through the Lord's eyes. He missed some opportunities to teach because he didn't believe that was his assignment. He would say to the person, "Let me introduce you to one of our teachers." Everyone should seize opportunities as they arrive.

On the other hand, there were several things Patrick thinks the team did very well.

They utilized outside resources such as Dr. Galyn Van Rheenan from ACU and Jay Jarboe from Sunset International Bible Institute to come in and evaluate where they were and where they were going. "Sometimes, team members get so wrapped up in the every day details that they develop tunnel vision and need a different perspective," Patrick said.

All team members had undergone psychological testing before going to Mexico and SIBI continues to provide that service on an as needed basis.

They felt the pulse of denominational mission works in the city. They studied their methods, evaluated what worked and what didn't, and compared attrition rates. They researched these before going and while they were on the field.

The team held two Partner Meetings for their supporters. They invited them to come to Guadalajara for a weekend in October 1999 and again in February 2002. For the meetings, the team prepared a detailed agenda and packets of information that included goals, strategies, and results.

They developed a specific and systematic plan to move a young Christian from infancy to effectively serving as a small group leader. The courses included: Bible study, doctrinal foundations, daily homework, scripture memorization, ministry assignments, evangelistic training, and practical small group ministry. They designed a series of courses to be covered in eighteen to twenty-four months.

Patrick and Malissa have been married for eleven years and have three children. The first was born two months before going to Guadalajara, the second was born there, and the third conceived there. Patrick believes God blessed their marriage while in Mexico. To counteract his self confessed workaholic personality, they developed the habit of his rising early to have time alone with God. Then, he would care for the children from seven to eight in the morning to allow Malissa personal time to journal, pray, study, or whatever she needed to do for her spiritual well being. That personal time provided Malissa purpose and an unobstructed daily presence with the Lord. They feel strongly that this makes both persons stronger and helped them grow in their personal walk with God. "It's necessary for me to maintain balance now while working 55 hours each week with AIM," he stated.

When asked if they experienced reverse culture shock when they moved back to Lubbock, he replied, "We still are. It's more encompassing than culture shock." They expected difficulties when they moved to Guadalajara and dealt with them. They weren't as aware of the impact of the shock of returning to their former culture. When in Mexico, everyone wanted to touch their children. They weren't sure how to react to that attention in the street. On their return, they wondered why Texans didn't notice them. Patrick describes his feelings, "Returning from the mission field is somewhat akin to coming back from church camp where you were on an emotional high. The let down comes in waves at unexpected times." He says Malissa is very frugal and hasn't bought anything for herself since they have come back. However, recently she called Mexico and talked for two hours. She just felt the need to reconnect to the people there.

In recent months, they have experienced many changes. They took a huge salary cut when they came back. Their oldest child started kindergarten after having changed countries and cultures. They wonder if she is acting out or if this is part of reverse culture shock. The four year old wants to know why they don't sing right in church (he means in Spanish instead of English). They are fortunate in Lubbock to have friends who have experienced reverse culture shock. One elder at Sunset is providing reentry counseling. He brought things to their attention that they hadn't yet realized they were struggling with. "Knowing is half the battle," Patrick said. "I don't want to use that as a crutch, but emotions are real." He is thankful for their wonderful marriage relationship, as that has provided a rock during all the changes.

Patrick loves working at AIM and is convicted that the program is important to spreading God's word. He got his start in the program, returned from his first mission experience for more training, went again to the mission field, and while in the field invited AIM students to come and work with them. "I'm doing mission work now while working at AIM," he states. "I serve in God's pipeline preparing missionaries for life. AIM is a proponent of life changes. It prepares young people for a life in missions, but whether they continue as missionaries or return to secular work, they will impact people's lives. AIM has been preparing students for thirty years, and its program is the single largest contributor of short-term missionaries. Over 1500 people come through AIM and over 1200 have gone to 140 nations. At any given time, at least 50 AIMers are working in foreign fields and another 50 are in training with a staff of 25 unpaid ex-AIMers. Working with AIM students is being involved with lost people," Patrick stated.

Will the Sheaffers return to the mission field? He says, "It's open ended now. Obvious this (AIM) is where God wants us now. If He wants us to go back, He will open a door. Until then, we will prepare and train short term and life long missionaries."

When the Sheaffers returned to Texas, they lost 75 percent of their support. Churches want to support cutting edge international mission works, but unfortunately, some don't appreciate the need to prepare missionaries. All of AIM and SIBI staff must raise their own support outside of the Sunset congregation.

"Churches in some ways idolize missionaries, but many pay them like paupers," Patrick said. "Instead of giving missionaries almost celebrity status, they should realize that Matthew 28 is universal in scope and not limited to professional ministers. Many churches aren't living the value of the Great Commission. They don't live preaching the word. Surrendering ourselves to the Lord Jesus and allowing Him to be an outflow in everything we do or express is a lifestyle decision. The need is real. People are dying all around, the workers few, and the time is short. Each of us should ask, 'How am I living, and how am I sacrificing?'"

Thought Provokers
1. Should missionaries take time to renew their spirits every few years? If so, what is a good interval between renewals, and how long should the renewal period last?
2. Is the work of training missionaries equally important as being a missionary?
3. Should all mission works hold supporter meetings? If so, should the supporter meetings be in country or in the U.S.?

Chapter Four

Down Under

Based on an interview with Dwight Whitsett

$\mathcal{T}$he missionary bug bit two Odessa, Texas children as they listened to exciting and inspiring reports from live missionaries in their home congregations. Then, one crowded evening during a Gospel Meeting, Dwight lost his heart when Brenda smiled at him from across the auditorium. Although they lived in the same city, they attended separate schools and congregations and did not know each other. They began dating and married three years later while college students at the University of North Texas.

Dwight began his preaching career while studying under a vocal music scholarship. He was leading singing at a small church not far from Denton, Texas. When his fellow student who had been preaching left, the congregation asked Dwight to preach every Sunday. The twenty-five dollars a week they offered looked mighty big to a college student. Before long, he recognized both a need and a desire to know more of God's word and enrolled at Sunset School of Preaching, which later would be known as Sunset International Bible Institute.

While a student at Sunset, the missionary fever caught fire and they began looking for a mission field. Dwight said it was hard to go through the school and not be interested in mission work. Unsure of his language skills, they decided to go to an English-speaking nation where they might be able to strengthen the church or plant a new one. After much study and prayer, they placed England, Nova Scotia and Canada high on their list. One day, out of the blue, a professor knocked on Dwight's door and said, "I think you need to go to Adelaide, Australia." The Whitsetts contacted Mel and Dot Ashby who lived in Amarillo, Texas and also were interested in Adelaide. After a great deal of prayer and deliberation, Dwight and Brenda decided to team with the Ashbys. The congregation that supported them at Sunset decided to continue to support them in Australia, but the Whitsetts had to raise their travel funds from other congregations. Six months after graduation, they with their three year-old son and nine-month old daughter loaded into a plane headed for the down-under continent.

When they arrived in Adelaide in 1967, they found the church that met in the center of the city was not interested in evangelism or growth. Adelaide is a large linear city, which runs along the Gulf of Saint Vincent. The Whitsetts and Ashbys moved to the northern section of the city called Elizabeth to plant a new congregation. When they built a building, they moved to nearby Para Hills.

Moving into a new culture can be overwhelming. Dwight remembers that Brenda suffered more than he. He had read several Australian history books and studied their culture before they left. She had two small children to care for and just didn't have time to make the same studies as he. They had difficulty understanding their neighbors. Catching onto the Australian dialect wasn't difficult, but many of their neighbors had migrated from the north and midlands of England. Understanding their accents was like learning a new language. Brenda had a really tough first two years, but after their furlough and another year, she was totally into the culture.

The Whitsetts let people in the city know about worship and bible classes by putting flyers in several thousand-mail boxes. But the people didn't come. After trying several other approaches to attract people, they found that inviting couples to dinner worked better than any thing else. Only after they built a relationship did people want to know what they had to teach. The Australians began to wonder why Dwight and Brenda were different and why they had come so far from their families. That's when they opened their hearts to learning about how God's message could make their lives better and more meaningful.

Looking back on these events several years later, Dwight wrote, "Let's face it. We haven't been very smart. People are not going to listen to the gospel simply because we are preaching it. We do a bit of advertising, get in our building or some other auditorium, and expect people to beat down the doors to hear our wonderful speeches. Alas, it has never worked that way and it never will! People listened to Jesus because he loved the souls of men and women and they knew it. He proved his concern by the deeds of kindness he performed. He, and those who first followed earned the right to be heard. Jesus, his apostles and disciples, validated the gospel by their deeds. We still need validation. We still have something to prove." (*The Urgent Revolution*, by Dwight Whitsett, Somerset Road Press, Dallas, Texas, 1997)

Ivan Stewart led a campaign in the seventies that resulted in seventy-six conversions. Severe emotional problems made many of these new Christians initially open to the gospel. Their presence brought a new dimension to Dwight's ministry, counseling. Through God's help, Dwight and the new disciples were able to work through their problems and most continued to walk in the light.

Another outreach tool that proved effective was a five-column-inch article Dwight wrote for the Saturday newspaper. Several people read the articles and then contacted Dwight. Many who became leaders in the church first met the Whitsetts through this media. One responder attended the Macquarie School of Preaching in Sydney, New South Wales and returned to work with Para Hills.

"Accidental mission work" is the term Dwight uses for the outreach program that resulted from new Christians reaching out to their friends. This outreach became one of the driving forces behind the growth of the church.

The Adelaide congregations often met together for fellowship. Each set its midweek meeting time on a different day so Christians could visit other churches and still meet with their own spiritual family.

In the early days, the church in Elizabeth met in a rented hall for Sunday morning, but it was unavailable on Thursday nights. The Whitsetts thought that was a tragedy. When the church was small, they met in one home for midweek worship. As the church grew, they had to meet in four homes, so they decided to build a building in nearby Para Hills. It was still under construction when Ivan Stewart led the campaign. When they realized how many were being converted, they had the builders knock down the brick walls, which were about knee high, to expand the auditorium and add additional classrooms.

Before the team went to Adelaide, they knew to not build something that the Australians would not be able to sustain after they left. They encouraged the congregation to start a building fund and purchase land. The Elizabeth church never solicited funds from American congregations. When they borrowed money from a United States loan company, they made all the payments themselves as they had determined to make and keep the building project their own.

About three months after moving into the building, people came to Dwight saying that something was missing. They missed the warmth that existed in the Thursday night home meetings. Dwight's attitude was, "You'll just have to get used to this." Today, he recognizes the value of the small group meetings for growth and outreach. Many people, who would not have come to a building, met the Lord in the midweek home bible studies. He encourages his students to read everything they can on cell groups and small groups.

The church continued to grow. They added their own bus program, the only one in Australia. By the time the Whitsetts left, average Sunday attendance was about 150, which made it one of the largest in Australia. They had appointed elders and deacons, supported their own Australian preacher, and ran the only bus program in the continent.

When a visiting preacher came through the city, the congregation would ask him to conduct a "Gospel Mission," which was the same as Gospel Meetings in the U.S.A. Those were always good times and good outreach, Dwight remembers.

"A mentor would have been a tremendous asset," Dwight said. Some of the visiting preachers had more experience than Dwight, but most didn't have mission experience. Still, talking to men who had served in the pulpit was uplifting and helpful. That's one of the reasons Dwight is now sharing his experience with students at Sunset International Bible School. He wants to provide the training that he didn't get. After the SIBI student graduates and goes to the mission field, Dwight maintains contact to provide experienced counseling. Continued contact is vital to young men and women working in foreign fields struggling to teach God's word effectively. Advances in technology enable rapid, cost-effective communication anywhere in the world. When Dwight and Brenda were in Australia, airmail letters took a week and phone calls were incredibly expensive. They mailed audiotapes back and forth in order to hear family members' voices.

Leadership training was primarily accomplished through teaching and preaching from the pulpit accompanied by encouraging those who demonstrated a talent in some aspect. Dwight helped those who showed a skill at one-on-one teaching find opportunities. Those who wanted to preach were placed in the pulpit at every opportunity. He laments that he would have been a lot more proactive in training if he had only known what he knows now.

The Whitsetts came back to the U.S.A. on their first furlough after two years in the field. Afterward, they came back every three years. Brenda had to come back once when her dad had a heart attack. Fortunately, he recovered. Their supporting congregations provided working and travel funds as well as for Brenda's special trip. Dwight didn't enjoy the furloughs. They always had to raise travel funds and replace some supporters that had stopped sending funds. "Furloughs were tough times," he remembers. They had become immersed in Australia's culture and considered themselves more Australian than American. Coming home was necessary to maintain support, but it wasn't a pleasant experience. One year, during an oil crisis and a bad economy, they lost considerable support. It took six months in the States driving more than 9000 miles to replace the lost funds. Those six months not only drained them physically but spiritually. Their co-worker held the work together in their absence. But Australia was their home and their mission, and they were anxious to return.

From the very beginning, they had the goal of transferring ownership to the Australians and worked toward that goal. Deciding on when the time is right for a missionary to leave is a difficult matter. Dwight often advises missionary students, "Don't leave before it is your time to leave. Get some help in determining when that time is." After ten years, he thought the time had come for them to leave. Elders had been appointed, a man had been trained at a preaching school, and the work was paying its own way. Yet, looking back, he feels that if he had stayed a little longer, he could have eased the transition for them.

After the Whitsetts left, many of the leaders moved over the years for various reasons: jobs, families and so on. The leadership training had not persisted, and that left them open to divisive teaching. Eight years after Dwight left, a leadership vacuum developed, and a church-splitter from Western Australia came in and divided the congregation. The new preacher sought to elevate his own authority and power and ignored the scriptures. One major issue involved the question of drinking wine during meals. South Australia is wine country, and in their culture, many drank wine with their meals. When the new preacher began preaching that it was sinful and wrong, the members asked for scripture. He couldn't give one, but continued to proclaim it as sinful and wrong. Strangely, the preacher had most of his trouble with a teetotaler. Dwight's opinion, when he recently met the preacher for the first time, is that he is power hungry. Several of the members said he had toned down a lot, but it wasn't obvious. Through the years, the preacher made some major changes, and he now accepts everything and anyone. Dwight said, "As so often happens, people who are extreme in one direction swing to the opposite extreme instead of stopping in the middle." About sixty people now meet in northern Adelaide. Several people went to other groups when the split occurred.

Dwight and Brenda have maintained a relationship with the church and have tried to visit as often as they could. While working as a pulpit minister after their return to the U.S.A., they visited every other year. Brenda became very ill after their trip in 1981, and that prevented their visiting for a while. They felt good about their 1981 trip and considered the congregation's attitudes and excitement level great. Then the church splitter arrived and the work began to falter.

Now, the Whitsetts' goal is to spend three to four months in Australia every year to encourage and train leaders. Having the necessary travel funds is a continuing problem in meeting this goal. All Sunset International Bible Institute staff must raise their own support for living and travel expenses.

Dwight is encouraged with merger discussions between the Salisbury congregation and the Adelaide Church of Christ now in progress. The Adelaide congregation is an International Church of Christ with about thirty-five members. They are enjoying their new freedom as a result of the loosening of that organization's control. Both congregations could benefit by a merger as Adelaide would bring evangelistic enthusiasm and the Salisbury congregation would bring mature leadership.

Why did the Whitsetts come back to the States when they did? Dwight said, "All the signals that missionaries looked for said it was time." Elders had been appointed, the congregation was paying its preacher, the bus program was going good, and the building payments were on time. The Whitsetts worried about their children's education, as the Australian public schools in their area were terrible. This was before the days of home schooling. The private schools were just too expensive for their missionary salary. Their families in the States continued to pressure them to bring the grandchildren home. In spite of this, Dwight didn't want to leave Australia. He wanted to move into a new category like an advisor and mentor or start a new work in a different city.

Six months after arriving in America, he knew he had made a mistake. Although he tried to raise support and return, it never happened.

The reverse culture shock they experienced on their return to the States was far worse than moving to Adelaide. The Whitsetts didn't realize how wasteful Americans are until they returned. Australians conserve everything and are careful with resources. They take excellent care of their cars and drive them until the wheels fall off. Americans seemed to change cars every year or two whether they needed to or not. But the biggest shock came from his work as pulpit minister. He taught and acted as he did while a missionary, and the church grew by about a 100 members in two years. His independence and evangelistic focus, which had served him well in the mission field, irritated the congregation's leadership. Eventually, he realized they wanted a pastor instead of an evangelist. Although he worked for the next twenty-two years in pulpits, he always felt like a misfit.

Many things had happened in the United States while they were gone that they never heard of. The Australian news covered the major happening in the States, but minor things went unnoticed. In fellowships, talk about TV shows the Whitsetts had never seen and news events they didn't know made them feel like outsiders. They had three children when they returned, all with Australian accents. The kids worked diligently to lose the accents so they wouldn't sound different, but all of the Whitsetts used a lot of colloquiums Americans didn't understand.

Dwight tells his students, "Think about making mission work a lifetime endeavor. Why not? If you can educate your kids and aren't having major problems, you may be much happier and productive there." He's not sure they're listening. He wishes he had stayed. The split might still have happened, but he feels he could have made a difference by being there.

When asked to list the primary things future missionaries should know, Dwight responded with the following.

Teaching the gospel eventually boils down to one on one. The missionary may attract some people through mass media and campaigns, but real conversion and discipleship come from one on one.

Make disciples. Take young men and disciple them. Take the time to train and develop these disciples. If he were to return, Dwight would set his goal at making twelve disciples and teaching them to make twelve more.

Don't try to do everything yourself and be careful not to neglect your family. It's easy to let work absorb all your time, and a common problem among missionaries is neglecting their family. Dwight emphases that it is stupid to neglect your family, as they are your responsibility, your support base, and critical to your staying on the mission field.

Present the message just as simply as you possibly can. Put all of your notebooks from school on a bookshelf and use them only for reference purposes. Dwight says he initially preached over the heads of people and was shocked to learn that wasn't what they needed.

Don't complicate mission work. The big problem is finding out what not to do. The missionary must go to the culture, immerse himself or herself in it, learn the language as soon as possible, and begin building relationships with people.

Today, Dwight serves at Sunset International Bible Institute as Missionary Coordinator for Oceania, Internship Coordinator, and teaches courses in advanced missions.

Thought Provokers

1. We need to earn the right to tell others about Christ's gospel? If so, how can we earn it?
2. When is the right time for a missionary to leave the new church plant?
3. How can people from supporting congregations ease the missionaries reverse culture shock? Or can they?

Chapter Five

Out of Africa, Into Australia

Based on an interview with Tim Pyles

*B*eautiful and bewitching Australia is described in the first book of the encyclopedia set that an earlier missionary family left in Monrovia, Liberia, West Africa. Ten-year-old Tim Pyles didn't see much TV or hear much radio, or watch many movies. He read what-ever he could get his hands on, and the old encyclopedias were available. The country down under with its unusual animals fascinated him, and he promised himself that one day, he would see the island continent himself. Little did he know then that God would one day lead him there to share the gospel message.

In 1973 and 1974, Tim was in Monrovia with his missionary dad, Willard, his mom, Shelby, and his eleven-year-old sister, Karen. Willard Pyles had been a local preacher and an educator before responding to the missionary call. That response expanded his children's world as they entered a new and foreign culture. They attended American Cooperative School, which was populated mostly with government workers' and missionaries' children. Although English was the official language of the school, it was truly international with fourteen to fifteen different nationalities represented. Tim not only sampled several cultures at school, he experienced the Liberian culture first hand while traveling with his dad to various churches outside Monrovia. Many times they walked to the churches, as there were no roads. He called it a "wonderful adventure."

The church in Liberia didn't look the same to Tim as it had in Kentucky. He recognized the common faith, but the poverty and values were greatly different. Watching and listening to his father teach and tutor the Liberian Christians was great training for Tim.

After two years, the Pyles family returned to Kentucky where Willard resumed congregational ministry. Later, he taught and served with the administration of International Bible College, now known as Heritage Christian University. Almost every Sunday, he found time to preach at various congregations. He also continued to be involved with domestic evangelistic campaigns and several short-term mission trips to Liberia, Nigeria, Australia, and other places. His zeal for evangelism transferred to Tim.

Tim graduated from high school in Montgomery, Alabama with full intentions of majoring in Forest Engineering at Auburn. Only a few nights before he was to leave for the university, he spent some sleepless nights wondering if he should change his major. After much prayer and internal searching, the Forest Service lost a good man as Tim decided to enroll in Bible at Alabama Christian College, now known as Faulkner University. His interest in missions intensified and after a year he transferred to Lipscomb University to major in Bible and Missions.

Joe Gray, a professor at Lipscomb, directed a program entitled "Project Good News," and Tim enrolled. Any student could enroll if they would commit to spending two years in the mission field working under an experienced missionary. While in school, the student had to take certain required courses, most of which were already woven into Tim's degree program.

Australia still fascinated Tim. One day while in Dr. Gray's office, he noticed a letter from Australia and asked the secretary if he might have it when she finished with it. Tim began a two-year correspondence with the missionary who had sent a request for help. Through the mails, they built a strong bond long before Tim arrived.

After receiving a B.A. in Missions in June 1985, Tim spent two months raising support. Several churches ranging from Georgia to Ohio joined with his sponsoring congregation, the Westvue Church of Christ in Lewisburg,

Tennessee. Project Good News required its members to go for two years on subsistence wages with no return visits until the two years were completed. That meant no car, no high living, and few new clothes.

Although they had corresponded for two years, neither Tim nor the missionary had thought to send a picture. So, when Tim got off the airplane in Brisbane, Queensland, Australia, he just looked for someone who looked like they were looking for someone. Soon, they were on their way to Gympie, a small city about 100 miles north of Brisbane situated on Queensland's eastern Sunshine Highway.

He soon settled into working alongside the resident missionary who had been there for about three years. Tim's main responsibility was personal evangelism. He found many sincere seekers among the town's thirteen thousand people. Most religious people claimed to be either Anglican or Catholic, although most were only nominal members. Typically, his students required a long time of intensive study before they were ready to receive Christ's message and His demands for their lives. After conversion, they needed a lot of support and disciple time as they fought the Devil's snares in their new life commitment.

Tim also worked with the congregation's youth. He planned several "bush camps" for the youth and their families. A member let them use his property for the camps, and Tim remembers the excursions as really roughing it. They had no facilities of any kind, so all campers had to bring their own sleeping and cooking gear. Over a hundred people would bring their tents, endure "bush showers," and prepare their own food just so they could enjoy the games and fellowship of fellow Christians. Every night, they listened intently to the preaching, and each day engaged with great enthusiasm in the games and class times.

Fellowship was very important, as the nearest congregation was two hours away in Brisbane and the next, three hours to the north in Bundaberg. Several would drive sixteen hours to Sidney for the annual Blue Sky Bible Camp. Today, there are additional congregations closer to Gympie.

Australia is a big, open country and some members drove many miles to attend worship. Tim has fond memories of one family who drove ninety miles one way. They were always there for bible classes at 10:00 AM and worship following. In recognition of the remote locations of some of the members, the congregation ate together after morning worship, and then met again until about 3:00 PM.

Every other Friday afternoon, Tim would catch the bus to ride ninety miles. The family would meet him and drive him to their cattle property. They were eager to study the scriptures and he would stay and study Friday and Saturday nights before rising early on Sunday for the long drive back to Gympie.

Tim considers Australia as culturally similar to the United States. Though the two countries share the English language, certain expressions and idioms were new to him or carried significantly different meanings. Seasonal differences, such as hot on Christmas and cold on the Fourth of July, required some attitude adjustments.

Tim stayed in contact with his supporting congregations though monthly newsletters. Email was not available at that time. Tim says that email may be one of the greatest technological advances for missionaries. Now, communication between supporting congregations and the evangelist can occur in seconds instead of weeks.

When Tim left, Gympie's Sunday attendance averaged about sixty. He went back to Lipscomb for graduate school with the intentions of returning to plant a new congregation in Nambour, which is located about half way between Gympie and Brisbane. However, he met a young woman he decided to spend the rest of his life with. After discussing mission work thoroughly, they selected Hawaii as the place to began their ministry together. They later returned to minister in the U.S. mainland and eventually moved to Dallas, Texas. He presently ministers to a growing congregation in Plano, Texas

Tim has restricted his mission work to short-term trips and has visited several works in South Africa, Scotland, England, and Nigeria.

Culture shock hit Tim harder on his return than it did when he went to Australia. The much larger stateside congregations and the immensely greater affluence required major attitude adjustments. In Queensland, the pace of life was much slower than in the U.S.A. But what really hit him was the lackadaisical attitude many church members had toward evangelism. He wondered if the difference in attitudes concerning evangelism related to their length of membership. In Australia, most of the members were first generation Christians and their reasons for committing to Christ were fresh on their minds and hearts. The Americans, in many cases, were third and forth generation Christians.

Tim worked hard not to be overly critical of his American brothers. They had not been where he had been and had not experienced the thrill of seeing people's eyes brighten when they first understood God's good news. Tim struggled with the cross-cultural danger of trying to impose foreign culture on his brothers. He counsels those returning from the field to not criticize their brethren for not understanding what they themselves had to go abroad to learn.

Tim regrets that there is no longer a formal mission apprenticeship program at Lipscomb to encourage young people to dedicate two years of their life to serve with an experienced missionary in spreading God's word. Weeklong, spring break, or summer term campaigns are now vogue at the universities. These campaigns benefit both the ones going and the ones receiving, however, they just don't have the impact on the young people that a two-year experience does. The writer and Tim both lament that church of Christ parents, unlike Mormon parents, do not expect their children to dedicate two years of their lives toward spreading God's message.

Tim is a firm believer in apprentice training for new missionaries. "It eases the young missionary's transition between cultures and helps the younger person to better organize and to be more effective in his or her life's work."

Tim also encourages all young people to devote two years after college to the mission field. "Even if they never do anymore mission work, it will change their lives. There's no better time than before they marry and have children and when they are just beginning their life's work." And Tim is not just talking about Bible and Ministry majors. He's talking about students in all college and university majors. Beginning their independent life by taking the wonderful, liberating message of Jesus to the unbelieving world will positively impact their lives and make them better servants of God.

Thought Provokers
1. Why don't Christian parents encourage their children to devote two years toward missionary work? Should they?
2. Is it possible for second, third, or fourth generation Christians to catch the fever and enthusiasm of first generation Christians? What generated the enthusiasm?
3. Should young missionaries sign up as apprentices to more experienced missionaries before going to a field on their own? What are the pros and cons?

Chapter Six

Have Medicine, Will Travel

Based on an interview with Bill and Owana Kidd

*T*he Kidds were living the good life in Ada, Oklahoma in 1967. Bill worked as Technical Director at the School of Medical Technology Technicians and served as an elder at the University Church of Christ. Owana was busy being a wife and mother to four energetic children, while spending as much time as possible in church activities. When some of the congregation joined the Exodus movement to plant churches in the northeastern states, it triggered a realization in the Kidds. They decided to move to an area where the church was weak or nonexistent and Bill's training as a Medical Technologist with graduate degrees in microbiology might be in demand.

First, Bill went to work for the Reynolds Army Hospital in Lawton, Oklahoma. Before long, he transferred to the Pine Ridge Indian Reservation in southwestern South Dakota. Bill's primary task at the Indian and Native Public Health Hospital involved improving their medical testing laboratories. Young medical doctors sought his advice on how to best use the available testing to confirm their diagnosis as his fifteen years of experience complemented their medical training. The INPH presented a challenging situation, but soon, under Bill's guidance, the labs improved. The Indian and Native Public Health Hospital noticed and after about seven months, they asked him to work at their headquarters in Aberdeen, South Dakota. Dr Emery Johnson, Director of Native Indian Health, noticed his work and appointed Bill as his consultant to oversee labs in ninety-two Indian reservation hospitals across the nation.

During the next eight years the Kidds strengthened and planted churches in the neighboring towns. On Sunday, the Kidds drove seventy-two miles each way to plant a church in Sisseton, South Dakota. For a couple raised in Alabama and Oklahoma, the fierce South Dakota winters were daunting, but not overwhelming. The church met in the Sisseton courthouse a few yards from the jail, where odors of dust and beer greeted them on Sunday mornings. In time, the church grew to seventeen members. The Kidds also helped start West River Bible Camp and Black Hills Bible Camp. The latter camp hosted about two hundred fifty children, sixty percent of who were not from Christian families. They fondly remember the day over thirty children responded to Christ. The camp remains popular today with many children coming from Canada and other states.

International missions beckoned after they moved to Dallas, Texas and placed membership at Waterview Church of Christ. A local member, a dentist, spoke of his experiences in establishing a dental clinic at Nigeria Christian Hospital in Aba Abia, Nigeria. Not long after, a representative from Health Talents International of Birmingham, AL spoke regarding medical missions. The Kidds felt the call.

It took them a year to save enough money to send Bill to Guatemala City with Health Talents International in August 1992. He had refurbished surplus lab equipment and used it to set up a lab in Clinica Promisa, *the clinic of promise*, which the Zone 11 Church of Christ operated. Non-medical people taught about Christ as the patients waited to be seen. Bill trained a technician to operate the lab, but her tenure was cut short. She married the clinic doctor and retired to be a wife and mother. Owana joined Bill three weeks later and worked with the ABC children's program. Feeling they had made a difference in the Guatemalans' lives, they signed on for other medical missions.

Bill received an invitation to help a doctor in the Guatemalan mountains near Chocola. While there, Bill lived in a sheep pen complete with outdoor bathroom facilities, a large tree. One night something fuzzy crawled into his sleeping bag. Was he ever happy to find it was just a tomcat! The cat became Bill's sleeping partner for the rest of the trip. The host's only English was "lanch" which meant "do you want me to prepare a lunch for you to take today?" Mostly, his meals consisted of squash cooked on corn tortillas heated on a small piece of tin laid over a bed of coals.

Each day, Bill accompanied the doctor, who was also a preacher, on house calls. The mountain people earned their living by picking coffee beans and carrying them down the mountain in large bags attached to their foreheads with leather bands. They lived in brick houses made of mud scraped from the floor. Basically, the doctor's technique involved treating fevers with antibiotics. One evening, Bill, the doctor and his wife stopped at a restaurant to eat. Based on his experience and a cursory glance around the establishment, Bill expressed his concern about eating there. The doctor shrugged it off, and two hours later, his wife began vomiting with the classic symptoms of food poisoning.

On his third trip, Bill lived in a former coffee storehouse. He had been enjoying the novel Jurassic Park until he noticed large bats living in the top of the building. His friend still teases him about being "afraid to read." Another terrifying moment came on a mountain trail. Many of the mountain people believed that alcohol made their spirits float higher toward God. On Catholic holy days, they would gather at cemeteries to commemorate the dead by eating and drinking copious amounts of beer. One such day, Bill was returning to his lodging when he met a man weaving down the mountain holding a machete. The man grinned at Bill, who had treated several people with gaping machete cuts inflicted by drunken celebrants. Fortunately, the man weaved on by and Bill sighed, greatly relieved.

Bill switched focus to Africa, beginning with a trip to Bomso, a small village outside of Kumasi, Ghana, West Africa where churches of Christ operate a clinic. The local 550-member congregation also has a preacher training school, a sewing school for girls, and a World Bible School grading center. Bill trained eleven lab assistants for their clinic. At the graduation ceremony, several local dignitaries spoke and a TV station sent a camera crew providing excellent publicity for the church. Bill twice endured the piercing headaches, cramping stomach pains, unforgiving nausea, and chilling fevers of malaria. He diagnosed his own illness using the new blood analysis equipment he donated.

Other trips took Bill and Owana to Nigeria Christian Hospital in Aba, Abia, Nigeria, the one the dentist at Waterview Church of Christ had discussed. Bill carried surplus equipment he had repaired, set up a laboratory, and trained technicians. He taught them how to manufacture their own saline IV solution for a nickel per bag rather than purchasing them at the exorbitant price they had been forced to pay. But, culture prevented the widespread use of the IV solution. The two tribes served by the hospital had been enemies for years, and since one tribe made the solution, the other wouldn't use it.

Every morning, the staff met for a devotional before beginning a grueling day. Bill worked in a surgical clinic preparing the patients, and since, AIDS and venereal diseases were prevalent, he took precautions to protect himself and the surgeons. The team performed 137 surgeries during the month. When they left, people were still begging for treatment. Operating conditions were not ideal. Often during surgery, the electricity failed and they would complete the operation by flashlight. The non-medical workers taught waiting patients the good news about Christ and several were baptized.

The local officials appreciated their work and a senator invited them to his home for dinner. He wore a white robe and a bowler hat. When he said "Thanks" for the food, he removed the hat, but immediately put it back on to eat. The senator was a well-educated man and a gifted musician who entertained them with classical numbers on the piano

The International Executive Service Corp invited Bill and Owana to increase the output and improve the quality of the hospital laboratory in Dhaka, Bangladesh. The hospital is the largest diabetic treatment facility in the world, but their blood drawing technique dismayed the Kidds. Every morning, the technicians would number 2500 test tubes. Then they numbered the patients as they came in. If a technician placed the newly drawn blood in the wrong tube, every subsequent patient's blood would be mislabeled. Bill and Owana taught them time and motion management, but the technicians had great difficulty in adjusting.

As was their habit, the Kidds contacted the Dhaka church. Michael Shaw, the preacher, had previously been a freedom fighter during the liberation of Bangladesh from Pakistan. He said ninety-two congregations had been established in the country within a ten-year time. The Kidds couldn't visit them because an on-going civil war made travel within the city or countryside extremely dangerous.

Because of the danger, the officials housed the Kidds in a gated community and stationed an armed guard at the gate. The guard opened the gate briefly as their car approached and slammed it immediately after the car passed. Generally, a car equipped with an armed guard picked them up in the morning and deposited them at the hospital after clearing all personal from the area. Then in the evening, the car would be waiting when they left the hospital. The few times the car was late, Owana, a graceful, tall woman with silver-laced-black hair, had to endure the stares of the men. Americans were rare in Bangladesh and especially tall women. The men would come very close and look at her from head to toe. She felt they did that, because, although she was modestly dressed, she did not wear the flowing, concealing native garb.

Bill fondly remembers the hospital director's remark when he saw Bill allowing Owana to precede him through doors when they first arrived. The director said, in a derisive tone, that he would never allow his wife to walk in front of him because she was inferior. Before the end of the month, the director respectfully walked behind them both.

One of the few times Bill worried about his safety came while flying to Mabaruma, a village about 300 miles north of Georgetown, Guyana and reachable only by boat or small

two-engine plane. It is only thirty miles from the place Jim
Jones induced his followers to swallow poison-packed red
Kool Aid. On their flight, a doctor was explaining how they
would be treating more snakebites than sickness. About that
time, one engine failed and Bill could see nothing but snake-
filled jungles underneath them. The pilot told them not to
worry, he had had to land in a rice field only a few days
before and only the plane was damaged. The pilot steered
toward an alternate airfield, but when he arrived, drying rice
covered the landing strip. They managed to limp on into
their destination on one engine with several nervous praying
passengers.

The team established their medical clinic next to the
church building that had been constructed by placing
stripped tree trunks on a concrete slab and covering the roof
with banana leaves. Soon, patients flowed in. The dentists
asked Bill to give deadening shots to the waiting patients so
they could move them through faster. There were so many
needing treatment and so few dentists. One female patient
walked fifty miles for treatment and slept under trees at
night.

Each night, the workers gathered as many listeners as
possible and preached the Good News. Lanterns illuminated
the night meetings and malaria carrying mosquitoes
swarmed. Owana caught the dread disease. There were a few
chairs for guests while the locals sat on backless benches.
Children often sat in guest's laps. During the day, those
workers not involved with medical treatment taught the
waiting patients. After a few days, the workers made the
mistake of moving those who were already Christians ahead
of those who weren't. The workers wanted to get more
teaching time with the unbelievers, but some patients
resented being pushed back down the line. Two seventy odd
year old women from Georgetown, Guyanna taught and
roamed the countryside looking for anyone who would study
God's word.

Chimala Mission Hospital in Tanzania, East Africa
received equipment and supplies rounded up and carried to
them by the Kidds. Owana remembers that it took them five

days to get there. Mechanical trouble caused them to overnight in Milan, Italy without exiting the plane before traveling on to Rome for another night's stay. The last 500 miles were covered in a Land Rover.

A river flowed through the hospital compound and tropical plants made a beautiful sight. Soon they were at work setting up the lab equipment and training lab technicians. Bill lectured doctors on the new tests they could now use. Owana found working in the pharmacy rewarding.

Many Maasi people stand over seven feet tall. They are a proud people and feel superior to other tribes. Both men and women shave their heads. The women wear beautiful purple dresses and adorn themselves with silver jewelry. Some of the other tribes had an unusual method of decorating their ears. When they were very young, the parents pierced their earlobes and enlarged the holes with sticks. Many adults could loop their ear lobes over the top of their ears.

The Kidds were assigned a house complete with cook, housekeeper, and a night guard. Farmers had set fires in the surrounding mountains, and the fires drove many snakes including cobras into the compound. Some of the cobras could spit blinding venom and be accurate at a range of twelve feet.

Christian natives brought the Kidds stalks of small sweet bananas. Each night, after a grueling day's work, they would relax with popcorn and games.

The International Executive Service Corp and International Rotary wanted to set up a model blood transfusion center to be copied and used throughout India. The Kidds accepted their invitation and traveled to Delhi, India. While Bill installed the $500,000 of equipment and trained technicians, Owana prepared an instruction book complete with facility blueprints for the facilities. The blueprints were so well done that only the location of the toilets needed changing. The seats faced away from Mecca instead of toward it! This was the Kidds only trip where they were not able to locate and work with the local church.

When a medical team formed to visit Narobi, Kenya, the Kidds joined. The hospital and a school which taught automobile mechanics, computer science, woodworking, cooking, and dietary arts occupied five acres. The school had an excellent reputation with the government, often supplying choirs for official functions. The local Christians brought many street girls into the compound to feed and clothe them. A large number of Somalian refugees had come into Nairobi, and many lived by stealing and prostitution.

The medical team treated 1200 to 1500 patients during their fourteen-hour workday, and still many were left untreated. Owana fitted eyeglasses for numerous people who had never had glasses. Many praised God because they could see clearly. On their way back to the airport, the team loaded the extra supplies on the back of the bus. However, the road was so rough, that the bus had to travel very slowly and people stole everything stored there. Bill said he noticed an attitude that he described as "If I see something you have that I want and if I can get it, it's OK. It just shows I'm smarter than you." Unfortunately, this cultural attitude had penetrated the church.

When Partners in Progress called again, Bill joined a medical team headed to Colombo, the capitol city of Sri Lanka, an island located off the eastern coast of India. The island is beautiful and inhabited by handsome and beautiful people who neatly dress in bright colors. It is a vacation haven for Europeans although a long civil war has left many inhabitants in a state of poverty. Five congregations of the church of Christ are there, but four do not fellowship one. Five years previous, one preacher wrote to the government to complain about the acts of another. The one charged was exported and the riff developed. Bill McDonaugh, Partners in Progress, hoped to use the clinic to bring the congregations together again, but was unsuccessful, although the clinic treated hundreds of patients.

Waterview Church of Christ supported missions in recently freed Lithuania. The Soviets had left the medical facilities in extremely poor condition. In 1998, Bill contacted an American-founded medical clinic to inquire if they needed a blood testing facility. They eagerly said yes, so the Kidds gathered up the necessary equipment and supplies with the hope that the missionaries as well as Lithuanians would receive better medical treatment. They spent a month setting up a facility for clinical chemistry, hematology, and kidney function tests. One of the technicians trained was a member of the church. While there, the Kidds taught at the local church and encouraged the missionaries. Prior to the trip and after, the Kidds gathered and shipped two twenty foot and two forty foot containers of medical supplies and equipment valued at over three million dollars. Local Christians distributed the supplies to hospitals, nursing homes, and paramedics. A Lithuanian congressman facilitated the first shipments. To show his appreciation for the aid, he invited the Kidds to participate in the 750th birthday of his city. With most of the inhabitants, he and the mayor publicly recognized their service.

Partners for Progress invited the Kidds to join a medical mission to a clinic about two and a half hours from Phnom Penh, Cambodia in February 2003. Their day began early. They breakfasted about 7 AM, arrived at the clinic at 10:30 and got back home about 6:30 PM to eat, shower, and rest so they could repeat the same schedule the next day. During the two weeks, seventy were baptized and two congregations planted.

The Kidds were astounded at the ignorance of the people concerning world affairs. They had no idea that man ever walked on the moon. Communist Khmer Rouge forces had slaughtered almost all of the educated people in the 1970-1990's along with about two million others. Out of thousands of Cambodian doctors working before blood flowed in Pol Pot's killing fields, only about fifty survived in Phnom Penh.

The Cambodian villagers are very poor and without medical resources. Yet they treated their American guests politely and respectfully. The local churches passed the news about the medical clinic to friends and family and hundreds came.

The Kidds are following Partners in Progress' plans to construct a medical and educational boat to ply the Mekong River. The boat will serve as a base from which to medically treat and preach the Good News to the people along the great river.

Stay tuned. The Kidds are already planning their next trip. They have more time to work for God since their retirement and are using it to glorify His name. They thank God that He has shown them a way to use their talents to further His Kingdom throughout the world.

Thought Provokers
1. How can one best couple humanitarian aid with the Great Commission?
2. What other professions, other than medical, can effectively be used in mission work?
3. How much does a short time worker have to know about the specific culture of the mission point before they can be effective?

Chapter Seven

Life-Changing Lessons Learned in Africa

by Glenn Rogers, Ph.D.

*G*lenn Rogers, along with his wife, Glenda, and their son, Zechariah, served as missionaries in Nigeria, West Africa in 1996-1997, where Glenn was an instructor in Bible and Ministry at the Nigerian Christian Bible College. After returning from Nigeria and completing two advanced degrees in Intercultural Studies, Glenn accepted a position as Professor of Missions and Multiethnic Ministry at the Center for Christian Education, in Irving, Texas. He graciously consented to writing this account.

I had been in Nigeria for about six weeks. The newness was beginning to wear thin around the edges. I was teaching a class on Paul's letters to the Corinthians and the Thessalonians. There were about eighty students assembled in the chapel area, a large concrete slab with a tin roof over it. It was an open-air affair—no sides. At 8:30 in the morning it was already hot and sticky.

I don't remember what occasioned the question, but it had to do with why bad things sometimes happen. Of course, in the context of the African world view the question was asked from the "who" point of view rather than the "why" point of view. For Africans there are no accidents. Bad things don't just happen. Someone causes them to happen. They constantly ask, "Who caused this to happen?" because in their world view it is vital to discover who has been offended, or who is angry, or who is trying to cause

49

them harm. Only when the person, being, or entity responsible for the harmful event can be identified can appropriate steps be taken to remedy the situation. Even Africans who are believers are vitally interested in, and constantly ask, the "who" question.

On this particular morning, I decided that I had been in Nigeria long enough, and that the students knew me well enough, that I could explain the truth to them. I asked them a question.

"How many of you have been riding a bicycle down the road and hit a spot of soft sand, lost control of the bicycle and fallen down?"

Eighty hands went up.

"All right," I said, "Who caused that to happen? Who caused you to lose your balance and fall down as you peddled down the road?"

Anticipation hung heavy in the air as they waited for my response. I paused for effect, scanning their faces as I did—eager, honest, sincere faces awaiting an answer to one of the most challenging questions of life: *what is the source of and solution to the problem of evil and suffering?*

Finally, triumphantly I announced, "Physics."

Just as all eighty had raised their hands a moment ago, all eighty of them now broke into uproarious laughter. It was as if what I had just said was the funniest thing they had ever heard.

Shocked at their response, I stood there confused, wondering what to do next. Somewhere in the recesses of my mind I decided, as all good naturalistic, scientifically oriented Western people inevitably do, that I had not given them enough information. Once they had all the pertinent and accurate scientific information they would see the truth of what I was explaining to them.

As the laughter died down, I began again. "Think about it," I said. They settled down immediately, realizing that I was now about to give them the answer they needed. "You're riding down the road," I said. "You've been riding on hard packed dirt and you are going fast. Then, suddenly, as you round a bend in the road, you hit a spot of soft sand.

The rotation of the front tire (I gestured, illustrating the rotation with my hands—I was animated) suddenly slows and, because of inertia, you are thrown forward. You try to maintain your balance, but cannot. The front wheel wobbles. One of your feet flies off the pedal and you fall."

The students were frozen in anticipation.

"Now why did that happen?" I asked. There were a few nods. "You were moving alone smoothly. There was your speed, the rotation of the wheels, your weight. Suddenly you hit the soft sand and slowed."

More nods. They all understood. It was a common experience.

"Speed. Inertia. Weight. A sudden slowing. A loss of balance. Gravity. You fell. Right?" Everyone nodded. "So why did that happen?" Again I paused, though not as long. "Physics," I said again. And again they broke into laughter.

What was going on here, I wondered? I had explained all the facets of the problem. I had put all the pieces of the puzzle together for them. Why were they laughing at me? I did not understand. So I asked them, "Why are you laughing at me?"

From the back of the class came the strong voice of one of the senior men in the class. "Why are you telling us physics did it?"

His question stopped me cold. Of course, I had told them physics had caused the bicycle accident because that was the way my Western scientific, naturalistic world view had taught me to answer such questions. I had told them physics did it because that is what I had been taught to believe. Obviously, they had been taught to believe something else.

I realized that morning that I did not understand the people among whom I was working. Over the next two years I realized that there was a great deal that I did not understand. There were several things about the Nigerian people that were confusing.

One of those confusing things was the fact that they seemed to have no sense of time, as far as promptness or punctuality was concerned. They would come and go at such a leisurely pace that the concept of being "on time" was virtually nonexistent.

Another thing that confused us was that everyone seemed to be related to everyone else. Nearly everyone who introduced us to someone claimed that the person they were introducing to us was either a brother or a sister. How could that be?

A behavior that we found particularly frustrating was that when someone came by to see you, they were very hesitant to get to the point. Not only did they not seem to appreciate the concept of an appointment, when they finally arrived at your home, they wanted to sit and chat for the longest time before getting to what they came to discuss. This made productivity difficult.

Another concept that was hard for us to understand was the importance they placed on "family" decisions. Many times a person who wanted to become a Christian would delay their response, waiting for their entire family to respond. They had some need to respond as a group rather than as individuals.

They were also overly interested in the supernatural. Everything was demons and spirits, witches and curses. And it was impossible to talk them out of it! They were adamant in their belief that the world of the supernatural was real, that Satan and his servants were capable of causing problems for people. They would point to the book of Job and the ministry of Jesus and suggest that such things still happen today.

It was also difficult to convince them that we were not rich. In our particular situation our support was just a tad over $20,000 per year, plus a house to live in. Not much by American standards. However, in Africa we were able to get by. But rich? Come on, we were certainly not rich. The Africans, who made about $500 per year, were constantly asking us for help. Why did they not understand that we were not rich? We did have a car to drive while most of them walked, and we were able to afford to buy chicken and pork while most of them rarely ate meat. And we could afford coffee, tea and soft drinks while they drank water.

But did that make us rich? We had money for medicine when we were sick, and could buy new clothes (or just about anything else that was available) in the market. But did that make us rich? Most of the Nigerians lived in a one-room hut. We lived in an old house that had been built of sandstone brick in 1954. It had a living room, dinning room, a small office, a kitchen, two bedrooms and a bathroom with indoor plumbing. But did that make us rich? There was not a day that went by when someone did not come by and ask us for money.

Frustrating for Glenda was the requirement of having to carry a head covering with her everywhere just in case there might be prayer. Women in Africa are expected to cover their heads according to Paul's instructions in 1 Corinthians 11. The Nigerians approach biblical interpretation in a very literal way—in some cases. Women are required to cover their heads if there is prayer. Men lift holy hands when they pray. However, the Nigerians draw the line at practicing the holy kiss. Such a thing is simply not possible in their culture. They are as inconsistent as we are in choosing which commands of the New Testament to disregard as merely cultural and which ought to be required of all people in all cultures.

A related issue was that women could not wear slacks. In Nigeria, only prostitutes wear slacks. The culture is changing slowly because of Western influence. In cities where there is a university, some of the girls will wear slacks. But when they go home they do not wear them. Naturally, missionary women cannot wear slacks without causing serious problems.

Another cultural "landmine," as Glenda likes to call them, is that in public men and women do not touch. Men can walk down the street holding hands. So can women. In that context such behavior is not indicative of homosexuality. In fact, homosexuality is virtually nonexistent in Africa. Same gender contact merely represents friendship. But physical contact between men and women is not acceptable. For a man to touch a woman in public indicates that he wants to have sex with her. This becomes a problem (for missionaries) when our unconscious (American) habits kick in. In worship here at home it is not uncommon for a man to take his wife's hand (or even slip his arm around her shoulder) during the Lord's Supper. For us it is a sign of closeness. To the Nigerians, however, such behavior is scandalous. Touching in public is bad enough, but thinking about sex during the Lord's Supper! How immoral!

As far as our teenage son was concerned, his main frustrations had to do with having to adjust to home schooling and not being able to drive. He turned sixteen two weeks before we left the States for Nigeria. Driving in foreign countries can be very hazardous. Many missionaries do not do their own driving, choosing instead to utilize the services of a local experienced driver. That way, if there is an accident (which is taken very seriously and can be very expensive if there is an American involved) neither the missionary nor the mission work itself is in jeopardy. For a sixteen year old with a new driver's license to give up driving for two years was a major sacrifice.

Zach's other frustration was home schooling. It wasn't that he didn't like being taught by either Mom or Dad, it was just a different way of doing things that required additional adjustment.

He did well, however. Everyone on the mission team treated him like an adult, giving him two of the most important jobs in the compound: running the massive generator twice each day, providing us with electricity, and filling the water tower each evening so we would have running water.

By the time we left Nigeria we had discovered partial answers to many of our questions and had gotten over many (though not all) of our frustrations. We came to understand that the Nigerians simply think differently about many things than we do. We did not, however, understand why. We came to realize that they thought differently about time than we do. They have a different view of family and relationships than we in the West do. They think differently about the priority of relationships with people over productivity. Their view of wealth and sharing is different than ours. Their view of how the world works, especially when it comes to the supernatural, is very different than ours. And even if they are wrong about some of their beliefs regarding supernatural things, we must also acknowledge that we may have a few misconceptions ourselves. Answers to such questions are never simple.

One of the most important things we learned in Nigeria is that most of the time there are differences in the way people think about things. It is not a matter of whose cultural ways are right and whose are wrong. Most of the time, it is a matter of understanding the differences and acknowledging the validity of a perspective different from our own. Living in Nigeria was a marvelous, life-changing event (even with all of the difficulties and frustrations) that we will always cherish. We learned cultural and theological humility.

After returning from Nigeria I began studying missiology at Fuller Theological Seminary School of World Mission (now the School of Intercultural Studies). My very first course was Cultural Anthropology, taught by an anthropologist who had been a missionary in Nigeria. In every class he would tell a story or explain something from an anthropological perspective that would have me leaving class mumbling something to the effect that, "if I had known that before I went, I wouldn't have made that mistake." Over the four years I studied at Fuller (earning my M.A. and Ph.D. in Intercultural Studies) I had many occasions to say (or to think) "if only I had known that before I went." It was during my time at Fuller, studying missiology and anthropology that I began to understand the "why" of many of the things that had occurred in Nigeria.

This is important because before we went to Nigeria I thought I was ready. I thought I was well trained and qualified. Years before (in the mid 1970's) I had graduated from a well-known school of preaching where I'd had a course in missions. I had attended Pepperdine University. I had continued my schooling and had earned a D. Min. in Christian counseling. Just before leaving for Nigeria I read a book on missions in Africa. I had been preaching (at that time) for twenty-five years. I knew the Word. I could teach and preach. I thought I was ready. I was not. I'd had no anthropological training, no missiological training, and no cross-cultural skills at all. If someone had suggested that I was not fully prepared, I would have been insulted. I would have assured them that I was quite well prepared. But I was not.

What is my point? Most missionaries sent into the field by churches of Christ are not adequately prepared. Statistics indicate that the churches of Christ are among the top ten largest mission-sending agencies in the world. Yet most of our missionaries go into the field with little or no specific missiological or anthropological training. A college course or a few months at a special training center where former missionaries (who themselves may or may not have formal missiological training) teach some basic missions courses is simply not sufficient.

Church leaders who support missions must insist that missionaries spend the time to get advanced missiological (which includes anthropological) training. It may delay sending someone into the field for eighteen to twenty-four months, but it is worth the delay to have missionaries in the field who are well trained. Missionaries need training in mission theology and theory, anthropology, world view, contextualization, and cross-cultural communication. Cross-cultural mission, whether half way around the world or right here in our own ethnically diverse American communities, is the most important and challenging work we have to do. If we are to do it effectively, we must insist that our missionaries be adequately trained.

Thought Provokers
1. Is it necessary to understand how a person views life events (world view) before we can effectively teach them God's word?
2. Is the term "landmine" descriptive for cultural faux pas? If so, how do we find such landmines before we step on them?
3. What determines if we are rich or not?

Chapter Eight

From Belgrade to Moscow and Beyond

Based on an interview with Gary Jackson

*D*id the person who arranged the Youth Panel for the World Evangelism Forum at Sunset Church of Christ have any idea about the results? He probably sought God's help in selecting the participants before selecting Gary Jackson and Danita Edwards, but may have been unaware of the life changing events about to be set in motion. Both Gary and Danita had completed Adventures in Missions at Sunset earlier and been to the mission field.

After serving in Canada, Gary enrolled at Sunset Preaching School, now known as Sunset International Bible Institute or SIBI. Danita had recently returned from Columbia. Love was born that day, and several months later they married, forming a lifelong mission team.

Long before the Berlin Wall crumbled, Bob Hare smuggled bibles across the Iron Curtain, organized humanitarian aid to Poland, and actively sought to spread God's word anywhere possible in the Soviet Eastern Bloc. When, in SIBI chapel, Hare passionately predicted that God would bring down the wall and open a way into Russia, the Jacksons determined to march through the break. Yugoslavia offered the only way to enter the Soviet Bloc at that time, so they, along with Ron and Linda Skorick, placed the capitol city Belgrade in their sights.

After completing Sunset's preaching school and graduate missions program, Gary, Danita and their nine-month-old son Joshua, along with the Skoricks and their four children flew to Belgrade in 1983. Garden Ridge Church of Christ in Lewisville, Texas oversaw the Jacksons and several other congregations provided financial support. All but one of the original supporting congregations are still supporting the Jacksons today.

When they arrived, one Christian lady met them. She had been converted while an exchange student to the United States. The team planned to convert Yugoslavs and let them take the gospel into Russia since Americans could not.

Although not as closed as the rest of the Soviet Bloc, the Yugoslavian government still forbade open evangelism. Gary and Ron had studied the Serbian language while at Sunset and enrolled at the University of Belgrade intending on using friendship evangelism to develop personal contacts while perfecting their language skills. They studied with a few Yugoslav students, but God opened the door in an unexpected manner. Several English speaking Africans studying on scholarship at the university proved to be much more open to the gospel. As the Africans began to study and accept Christ, they provided inroads by bringing Yugoslavian friends. One Nigerian student brought, through the years, sixteen to Christ.

The students came with varied religious backgrounds. Some didn't believe in God, so the Jacksons began with apologetics. Others believed the bible but didn't understand it. In those cases, they began with the creation, God's promises and fulfillment, His scheme of redemption, and His son, Jesus the Christ.

At first, they met in their homes, and later, as the church grew, moved to an apartment. Kevin and Linda Hutchins, also graduates of Sunset, joined them later and growth continued. The Hungarian Reformed Church had a building, but few members, so they began leasing it out. The church of Christ renovated the basement and used it for an office and meeting place. Later, when the building was destroyed, the Reformed Church moved them into another building so they could maintain the office and meeting place. The church still meets there today.

Since about twenty English-speaking Africans attended, they had two services, one in English and one in Serbian. When the economy worsened, the government eliminated the state sponsored scholarships and many of the Africans were forced to leave. Before the Jacksons left in 1993, Andy and Nell Bostich joined the team. The congregation had grown to about 50 members and had both Yugoslav and African leaders. Africans led the way at the beginning, and one of the strong leaders today is a West African.

When people converted, they enrolled in a disciples' class. Individual and group classes, for men and for women, were held in university dormitory rooms and member's homes. These classes were designed to mature the Christians and to provide them with leadership and evangelistic skills.

The new Christians often asked, "How long will you be here?" At first, the Jacksons answered, "As long as we are needed." The people said, "You will always be needed." So, in 1990, the Jacksons set 1993 as their target date for leaving. The next three years, they focused on developing the necessary leadership. The advance notice provided time for the congregation to accept that they were really going to leave and adjust. Even then, many members couldn't imagine that they would actually leave. In ten years working in Yugoslavia, they established a congregation that survived a civil war, NATO bombings, and radical changes in government. The congregation not only survived, it planted two other churches.

When the Jacksons returned, their children were in second and seventh grades. Gary and Danita wanted to give them a year to get a feel of what living in the United States was like. Gary served as a visiting missionary at Abilene Christian University. The one-year program provided them a sabbatical time of spiritual renewal. They also gained additional learning through graduate work and interaction with the faculty. While still in Yugoslavia, they had set their eyes on Russia, and hoped and prayed God would bring a team together during their sabbatical. He did.

In 1994, they went to Moscow with Tim and Rebecca Brimley. Terry and Lisa Harmon and Joyce Blake joined them later.

Gary's Serbian language skills helped them find an apartment and get it remodeled without an interpreter. Russian and Serbian are both Slavic languages, and although similar, are not the same. It took a lot of smiling, laughing, and turning to the phrase book and dictionary to communicate with the workers. Gary enrolled in Moscow Technical University and obtained a Masters in Russian Literature and Arts.

Before the team arrived, Let's Start Talking groups had been to Moscow and began a congregation in the early 1990's. Most of the members were university students. A congregation in Malibu, California had continued to send people to work with the congregation, while seeking someone to help mature the young Christians. The team hoped to do that, but soon, they recognized that this was not a good marriage. The young students had focused mostly on social relationships and thought the newly arrived Americans came to take over their church. After nine months, the team pulled out of the existing congregation and planted a new one in the large city. They continued to help the students hold Sunday worship. Eventually, the students disbanded their congregation and some came to the new church.

In Russia, they could evangelize openly. They tried several approaches, including street evangelism, correspondence courses, Let's Start Talking groups, inviting neighbors, advertising meetings, marriage seminars, and marriage enrichment. These all worked great for Christians, but didn't bring non-believers for in-depth studies. Let's Start Talking proved most effective as it provided neutral territory for people to comfortably attend. Let's Start Talking groups offered free English lessons to anyone who would study. They used Luke as the study guide and coupled friendship evangelism with language studies. It was an effective outreach tool.

In eight years, the church grew to an average Sunday morning attendance of 60-70 people. As more Russians were converted, the team set up a process whereby the congregation could select their own leaders. Although, no men were qualified to serve as elders, they promoted a leadership selection process similar to those American churches often used. During the process, Sunday morning messages taught Christian leadership and organization. The congregation looked through their number and chose five men to serve as spiritual leaders. These men continue to lead the congregation.

As they had in Belgrade, the Jacksons gave the members three-year notice of their intentions to leave. The people didn't really believe they would. "Why would you want to leave?" they asked. "You love us so much and we love you." Gary said it is important to give the congregation plenty of notice that you are going to leave. It's hard to leave, but, he stresses, it's like raising kids, you just have to turn loose and let them develop. Both times the Jacksons went to the mission field; they determined to stay for a minimum of five years, but stayed ten and nine years. They set goals and made plans. They thought that within nine to ten years, they could have the church matured where they could pull out. They prayed it would come together and in May 2003, they felt the time was ripe. Their daughter was graduating from high school that year and their son had already left for Harding University. The opportunity to serve as a visiting missionary at Harding sealed it.

The Jacksons are now planning to go to Beijing, China in the fall of 2004. When asked why he would go to another mission field, Gary smiled. "My visiting missionary position is only a one-year position. I really love it. My son and daughter-in-law are there. My daughter is a freshman. Yet we feel called to go." Gary is fulfilling a mission in service to God and man. He is at peace, knowing he has made a difference in world evangelism. He knows now he can and did. He is thrilled that they taught in two other cultures, interacted with Yugoslavs and Russians, and got to know them in their context. He enjoyed seeing how God gave each group a unique personality. He says it was good for the family, and the children feel blessed by the experience.

Sure, the children missed out on some things here in the States, but they received many other benefits. They had special opportunities, which many don't have. They speak Russian and often interact with Russian-speakers at Harding.

One of the great benefits of mission work is becoming close to one's fellow workers. On the front lines, Christians get close to loving Christians and support one another. They remain close and good friends with their coworkers. It was important to get out of the field long enough to feel comfortable going back. Now they eagerly look forward to preaching in China.

Culture shock is real. They feel that their studies at AIM and their cross-cultural experiences before they met and married helped them. It wasn't very bad in either Yugoslavia or Russia. Even so, they still had down times when they wished they were home in the States. Yet, they never felt so overwhelmed as to really plan on leaving the field. Culture shock engulfs some missionaries and they can't get over the hump.

Gary said, "Surviving culture shock is a learning curve, and the missionaries must recognize what is happening to them. It is a significant challenge to absorb a new culture, and it isn't easy. Everyone gets down and must work his or her way out. Having a close team is the best way to overcome culture shock. Hopefully, the team members won't all get down at the same time. One may feel low and complain while others encourage and boosts him or her up. Fellowship with team members is especially critical in the early days before one makes friends with the locals."

When they were in Yugoslavia, they tried to leave the country for a few days every three months. It was easy to visit Italy, Greece, or Austria for two days of shopping and get back for Sunday. On the short visits, they felt it easier to breath. Those were dark times in Yugoslavia, and shopping for western goods helped them escape the pressure. In Russia, they were older and could handle the culture better. Also, getting out of the country was more challenging. They still tried to take a winter and summer vacation on non-furlough years. The trips helped get their emotions back on track and revive their spirits. Family vacations where they spent good time together were always encouraging. For a few days, they enjoyed being alone and not always having people coming into their house.

Every two years, they came to the United States for two to three months to report to their supporting churches and to visit families. The team rotated furloughs so someone was always at the mission point. The time both team families left together was in Moscow during the time of transition. It allowed the church to see what it would be like when they were gone, and Gary felt the church benefited from it.

Gary said, "One of the most important things a person can do as a missionary is go. I'm a textbook missionary. Learning the language and culture are extremely important, however, I've seen God work in ways that are not textbook. People need to go even if they can't get the training before time. I've seen people do well who didn't have training. Sure, I've seen them make mistakes, but trained missionaries make mistakes too. If a person loves people and God, that overrides everything. Some people don't go because they aren't trained, and that's a mistake.

"A common mistake missionaries make is spending too little time preparing leaders," Gary said. "The missionaries go, work hard, and leave before developing a local leader. Too often, their work is like that of the man who built his house on the sand."

Gary thinks the idea that the new congregation needs a paid preacher is a mistake. If the congregation can afford one, it's great. But, putting local preachers on American salaries is a huge mistake. Let the people make their own decisions. If they want a paid preacher, they need to get one. Americans make a big mistake if they pick out a person to preach and decide what to pay without involving the local church. It has been proven to be a mistake with a few notable exceptions. It limits the local congregation and the worker when all decisions are made in the States.

"Too often, the missionary does not see the work through to a logical handoff," Gary said. "Missionaries sometimes make a three-year commitment and leave with no one to take their place."

"Some missionaries have isolated the church they helped plant and discourage fellowship with other congregations," Gary continued. "They seem to be afraid that through fellowship, a foreign teaching will taint the congregation. It is difficult for such a congregation to feel a part of the larger brotherhood."

When the Jacksons moved to Abilene Christian University or to Harding University, they did not experience the severe reverse culture shock that many returning missionaries report. He attributes that to training and experience. The second time has definitely been better than the first. Both times they have returned, they have had very good support systems at the two schools. They found good churches, good university staff, earnest prayer partners, and meaningful ministries. Sometimes people come back and get into positions where they don't feel they are making a meaningful contribution to the Kingdom. He remembers one missionary who took a conventional ministry position. He had a lot of busy work, but was isolated from people and wasn't impacting lives. He went into a deep depression and didn't recover for several years. "Everyone who returns will face difficulties with many things like telephone hookups, getting settled, moving into a church setting, and reestablishing a household," Gary emphasized. "The cost of this adjustment is frustration. Some move back into an unhealthy church situation and don't get support. I'm grateful to be on the receiving end."

One Chinese couple they taught in Moscow moved to Beijing, China, and the Jacksons visited them before going to Harding University. Currently, the Jacksons are formulating plans for moving there in the fall of 2004. One more place in the world they can share God's good news.

Thought Provokers
1.   What can a returning missionary do to reduce reverse culture shock? What can the supporting congregation do?

2. How important are reports by active missionaries in recruiting new people to take the gospel to foreign cultures? Do most churches provide those opportunities?

3. How long should missionaries commit to stay? Does it make a difference if they are planting or going to an existing congregation?

Chapter Nine

Long-Term, Short-Term Work

Based on an interview with Roger Thompson

Can one conduct a successful mission work and still spend most of one's time at a local congregation in the United States? Read the story of this work in the Ukraine and decide for yourself.

It all began in 1993 when Bill Fearris invited Roger Thompson to accompany him on a campaign to Donetsk, Ukraine. The elders of the Okemah, Oklahoma church of Christ agreed and bid him God-speed. Eddie Cloer led the big and successful campaign and several people came to Christ. Roger's concern was that people were being led to Christ, but inadequate follow-up was in place to bring them to full discipleship. David Deffenbaugh accompanied Roger on a second trip, and they birthed a unique partnership.

Neither Roger nor David could move to Ukraine, but having met the people, they felt a strong urging to do something. The new Christians needed good biblical based literature in the Russian language to help them grow and mature spiritually, and it was just not available. They determined, with God's help, to do something about that.

Roger and David asked Howard Norton, Grover Ship, and some other former missionaries to Brazil who were teaching at Oklahoma Christian University for advice. The Oklahoma Christian University group spent the first half-day relating everything they did wrong while in Brazil. Then, after lunch, they spent the rest of the day telling what they had done right. Roger said their input was fantastic and that he will be forever grateful to these good men.

After gaining support from their home congregations, the two men diligently begin raising funds to translate and print material into Russian. It was obvious that the task should be concentrated in Donetsk, since the technology and language expertise existed, and the hourly rate was much lower than in the United States.

In September 1994, they hired Helen Girsham, a Ukrainian Christian, to manage the Donetsk operation and to translate literature. She graciously used her bedroom as a translation office and warehoused the published materials in her parents' bedroom. As the work grew, they rented office space. In the year 2003, they purchased a facility.

Ukrainian law declares that a local congregation must be registered with the government and can only work within the city or district where registered. It cannot distribute literature, conduct public lectures, or invite foreign missionaries to conduct evangelistic campaigns in other cities.

However, the law did provide for a group of congregations registering a "center." As long as it is registered separately from any one congregation, it can establish educational, religious education, and charity organizations. The "center" has no authority over, nor the right to interfere with any activity of any congregation of the churches of Christ. Neither does it have the authority to direct the activities nor limit the rights of local congregations. Local congregations can make their own choice to work with the center or avoid it.

Roger and David scratched their heads for a name for the translation center and finally selected "Davaroh," a combination of their names and Helen Girsham's. After a few years, some people suggested Davaroh might be considered a missionary society, so Roger and David organized an informational meeting for interested and/or critical parties. The meeting took place in Searcy, and after Roger and David explained the requirements of Ukrainian law, the attendees left satisfied that no one wanted to control the mission work of United States congregations nor the operation of Ukrainian churches.

However, some friends advised them to replace the name Davaroh, as it might appear that the two men wanted to establish their own monument. After some research, they selected Blagovest, which means "good news" in Ukrainian. They registered that name with the government.

Blagovest's first endeavor was the establishment of the Libre-Press. Roger serves as President of Blagovest Board under the oversight of the elders at the Broken Arrow, Oklahoma church of Christ. David accepted the assignment of Vice President of the Blagovest Board, and also serves as Director of Libre-Press under the elders of the Tahlequah, Oklahoma church of Christ. At last count, Libre-Press had approximately one hundred separate pieces of literature available at no cost to Ukrainian churches. Since translation and printing work continues, the literature list continues to grow. To get the material, congregations only have to go by the warehouse and pick it up. There is no charge to local Christians. The material ranges from books to pamphlets to study courses to tracts. In the first seven months of 2003, they provided over 65,000 pieces of literature to Ukrainian churches, including almost 2500 bibles. In the year 2002, Blagovest printed and distributed more than 122,000 pieces of literature to over twenty-six congregations in the Donetsk region. They increased distribution in 2003 to more than 250,000 pieces.

There are about three thousand World Bible School students and over four hundred World English Institute students now being taught through correspondence throughout the Donetsk region. Everything is organized and maintained with computers. When the students are ready for personal interaction, the names and addresses are provided to their closest local congregation for follow-up. And now, the work has expanded to the United States. Some of the material is now being used to impact Russian and Ukrainian people in U. S. cities.

The printing work is expanding to meet the needs in other countries. In their first operation, 15,000 Russian bibles are being printed at an estimated cost of $2.28 each. When they first began printing, literature could easily be exported to Russia. Increasingly complicated custom laws between the two nations are now making export to Russia quiet difficult. Blagovest is setting up a printing operation in St. Petersburg to offset these regulations. The demand for a variety of materials is increasing.

As the work progressed, Roger recognized another need for the Donetsk region. Some men in outlying regions wanted to study the bible and could not travel to established schools due to work or financial factors. Many preached for local congregations and if they left, there was no one to fill the gap. The Blagovest Bible Institute was established with this need in mind. The State Committee of the Religious Affairs registered the Blagovest Bible Institute as the "highest spiritual theological school."

The Institute is the only school in Ukraine, and perhaps in the brotherhood, that combines distance and correspondence education with face-to-face lectures by the teachers. . Teachers, usually elders, preachers, or professors from the United States are selected for their areas of expertise. They prepare the material, which is then translated into Russian. The Institute mails the study materials and method guides to the student at the beginning of each course. He or she then studies the material at home or in groups. After writing the required test papers, the student mails them to the dean. At the end of each course, the teacher travels to Donetsk at his own expense and conducts a seminar at the Institute. At the seminar, the teacher reviews the covered material, addresses students' questions, and administers the final test. The Academic Dean controls the student's grades and sets the deadlines for a given course. The complete course of study takes about five years to finish.

The Institute provides the individual students free tuition, study materials, bibles and testing. The students must provide their own housing, food, and travel expenses. As of April 2003, eighty students from eighteen Ukrainian cities and five from Russia were enrolled.

When Roger first visited the Ukraine, their deep poverty touched his heart. On a trip in 1996, he asked about the welfare of a widow he had met the previous year. Dismay gripped him when he learned that she had died from malnutrition during the winter, not having adequate funds to purchase the correct foods. Many other widows lived in similar circumstances. The Orthodox Church would let them beg at their building's entrances if the widows would give a portion of their proceeds to the church. Their plight burdened Roger's heart, so he began a Widow's Fund. It supplies twenty dollars per month living expenses to those who qualify. Although the amount seems small to Americans, it can make the difference between life and death in Ukraine, especially during the harsh winters.

Orphans were, and are in desperate circumstances. One orphanage turned their children out into the streets to beg on weekends because they didn't have the money to care for them or to feed them. Roger couldn't get the words, *"Religion that God our Father accepts as pure and faultless is this: to look after orphans and widows in their distress and to keep oneself from being polluted by the world."* (James 1:27 NIV) Again, Roger sought help from brethren in the United States. They responded, and through Blagovest, the children at that orphanage now receive three meals every day of the week.

Christians in the United States financially assist over 3,000 children in twelve orphanages through Blagovest. Ukrainian Christians are teaching regular bible classes in several orphanages. They also take them to church and to youth camps so the children can learn about Jesus. Those local Christians who visit and play with the children provide a most important support function. There just isn't enough staff to adequately provide the attention the children need. Roger firmly believes that this benevolence work not only benefits the children, but new Christians as they learn to care for those less fortunate than themselves. Caring and taking action causes them to grow and mature in the nurture and admonition of the Lord.

Roger expresses amazement at what the Lord has done though Blagovest. He notes that Ukrainian orphans have more fundamental needs than those in America. Alexander, a local Christian, directs Kharov Orphanage where over 300 children live. He told Roger about a female worker praying that the children would have socks and shoes before the cruel winter began. When local Christians gave funds to purchase both winter boots and thermal socks for every child, she believed God sent them as angels.

Seven hospitals have also received humanitarian aid through Blagovest. American medical doctors have made visits to provide dental and eye care. Eyeglasses are expensive in Ukraine; so many children go without them. The American doctors have provided over 1600 pairs of glasses to children and adults.

This loving care demonstrated to the Ukrainian people has not gone unnoticed. Government authorities throughout the area recognize that the church of Christ cares for people. The mayor of Feodosia told Roger that the churches of Christ were their number one humanitarian aid provider for orphans, widows, and nursing homes. Recognizing that nursing homes are old and almost falling down, the mayor wanted to purchase a building and provide at least some of the elderly with decent care. He asked if the churches of Christ could help him. Roger received a sizeable gift from a fellow Christian and soon the entire $13,000 was in hand. All the donations came from private donors. When they presented the gift of supplies to the mayor, the Lord was glorified through TV, radio, and newspaper coverage. This new Nursing Home is scheduled to open in January 2004.

The humanitarian aid has also brought people to Christ. Blagovest serves as a conduit to bring the aid to Ukraine and to put local Christians in touch with the needy. The result is that Christ's name is taught and souls are saved. Many new Christians recognize Blagovest's role and write letters of thanksgiving to the overseeing elders.

Another need Blagovest is seeking to alleviate is family education. Like all nations formerly under Communist domination, Ukraine is burdened with alcoholics and broken families. Blagovest is developing a family video to uplift and provide direction to these lost and broken families. Rather than develop the video using only U.S. resources, Roger asked several Ukrainian specialists to get involved with Americans. The format for each video will be thirty minutes so it will be compatible with Ukrainian TV. They are also preparing a book that Roger hopes to place over 1,000 copies in local libraries. The material will be used in Christian summer camps as well as in the local congregations.

As a result of these efforts, the Ukrainian Ministry of Religion invited Blagovest to participate in a National Conference in Kiev in November 2003. Five people, Igor Kovlovsky, David Deffenbaugh, Lyle Asbyill, Marcia Lightsey, and Carol Bailey gave speeches designed to show the church as caring for people and intellectual in its pursuits to develop the country spiritually. The conference opened opportunities to enter three new regions, one of which has no churches of Christ. Several of the speakers were invited to return and lecture at four universities. They also were invited to submit articles for the national magazine *Panorama* and to place literature in the prestigious Center for Religious Freedom in Kiev.

On this same November trip, Tony and Marcia Lightsey conducted an area wide Family Conference in Donetsk hosted by Blagovest. Marcia is a licensed counselor from the Broken Arrow, Oklahoma congregation. Over 130 Ukrainians from across the region attended. Family communication is a vital topic and they are looking forward to more seminars on this subject.

Life is sometimes difficult for new Christians. For example, Igor worked in the government's Foreign Mission Department. One of their rules states that no one working in the department can be a member of any religious organization. The purpose of the rule was to insure impartiality to all religions. When Igor became a Christian, he lost his job. He accepted the lost with joy.

When Roger and David began their work, they decided that instead of raising money to send missionaries from the U.S., they would train local Christians. This has worked well in most cases, but not all. Sometimes, problems arise because the new Christians have not learned to trust their new brothers and sisters. After years of not knowing whom to trust, this is not surprising. A case in point is that of Ivan who served as treasurer for a congregation. He had been doing an admirable job, careful to document all receipts and expenses. When he left town for a few days and didn't leave anyone to manage the funds, others became upset. While he was gone, they replaced him. This caused a rift in the church, and required a lot of effort and teaching to undo.

Just as in Corinth, the desire for power and responsibility causes problems. In Ukraine, every organization must have a stamp. Nothing can be done without this stamp. The government issues the stamp and one cannot just go to an office supply and purchase another. It must be the official stamp. Seregy controlled one congregation's stamp, and when he became upset, he refused to use it or to return it to the congregation. The church tried persuasion, but when it failed they had to call in the police to retrieve it.

"Why should we expect problem free growth?" Roger asks. "We've never had it in the United States. Just as Jesus said, *'Woe to the world because of the things that cause people to sin! Such things must come, but woe to the man through whom they come!'"* (Matt. 18:7 NIV)

Roger believes that training national leaders in their own nation is proper for two reasons. First, many who come to the United States for training never return. Second, Americans should influence, but not control the new congregations. He says, "We shouldn't build anything we can't walk away from." He has no quarrel with those who send missionaries, and he says many have done an excellent work for the Lord. "There is no one way to do mission work," he states, "Blagovest has chosen this route."

Roger continues to minister at the Okemah church of Christ where he has served since 1985. They let him spend about half of his time raising funds and traveling to work with Blagovest. Usually, he travels to Ukraine about three times per year, although in 2003, he went four times. He and

David travel together once per year in the spring to guide and encourage the staff.

Roger and David have demonstrated that outreach to a foreign country can be effectively supplied and managed without living there full time. However, Roger emphasizes that their work would be ineffective without the work of several other congregations in Ukraine and their supporting U.S. congregations.

Perhaps we all need to consider what we can do with what God has given us and in the place we live.

Thought Questions
1. What is required to manage a mission work long distance?
2. Should the church tend to physical needs as well as spiritual? What are the pros and cons?
3. Is it important to get governmental recognition for the church? What does this mean for local Christians and non-Christians?

Chapter Ten

San Paulo, Brazil

Based on an interview with Michael Landon

Sao Paulo, a city built by coffee, is home to over 17 million souls. Established in 1554 when two Jesuit priests founded a small mission on the high plateau near the southern coast of Brazil, it is the fifth largest urban area in the world today. Unfortunately, only a small percentage of its population is part of the Lord's body. That fact drew Michael and Susan Landon to join the Sao Paulo mission team.

The Sao Paulo mission team had been in place for twenty-one years. Although its membership changed, its goal of teaching God's good news to the teeming multitudes remained constant. The team had established self-governing churches, and by the time Michael and Susan arrived, it only oversaw leadership training and the Christian camp. About a year after his arrival, the team disbanded and handed over all their authority to Brazilians. Several of the team members turned their energies toward planting new congregations.

Michael worked diligently to acquire a fluency in the Portuguese language. Having already been there on six short-term campaigns helped. He and Susan had studied the language for two years before going; however, he could only speak in the present tense when they arrived. He enrolled in a language school and hired tutors to gain proficiency. After five months, he could teach Sunday school, and after an additional two, he could preach. By the time the new congregation began, he did everything in Portuguese. At first, he would have the tutor review his lessons and help him translate them. Susan didn't have as much available time as Michael because she arrived in Sao Paulo pregnant. Their first child was born eight months later, their second after another fifteen months, and their third after another eighteen months. When they moved to Lapa, they worked only with Brazilians and were totally immersed in the language. They later took a course designed to improve the grammar of non-urban Brazilians.

Michael set the goal of planting and growing a new congregation that could financially support itself, lead itself and grow itself within eight to twelve years. Achieving that goal required more than baptizing people; it demanded transforming lives. He wanted each member to grow to his or her potential, whether as a Sunday School teacher, evangelistic Bible study teacher, elder, or evangelist.

He determined to evangelize whomever he could, but specifically targeted those he deemed the best raw material for an independent congregation, lower-to-middle class families.

The Continent of Great Cities emphasized that churches should be planted near crossroads. So, before the Sao Paulo team disbanded, Michael surveyed the city. The Lapa neighborhood served as transportation center for Sao Paulo's northwest quadrant. A million people could get there by bus without transferring. Next, he sought a place to rent that would be acceptable to the targeted group, i.e., safe for children, clean, and not demeaning. He found such a hall in a good central location and they began meeting. At that time, other than the Landons, only three members of the church of Christ lived among the 110,000 people; one couple and a single lady.

Evangelism developed around the web pattern. The first members talked to family members and co-workers about Christ and brought them to Michael. Soon, they were converting family units. When a person was converted, Michael would ask, "Whom do you know who would be interested in hearing about Jesus?" Then, when the new convert brought a friend or relative, Michael would insist he join the study saying, "You watch while I teach. Next time you can teach and I'll watch." And so, the men learned how to evangelize. Over the next six years, the church grew at a 25 to 50 percent rate bringing the membership to fifty adults and average Sunday morning attendance of about 90.

The Landons taught that teaching Sunday School was a privilege to be earned. Michael would start men teaching in people's homes and then transition them to classes and preaching. Susan taught women how to teach emphasizing the great privilege of training children. When a church member would transfer in, the Landon's waited until they knew and trusted them before allowing them to teach. They never searched for teachers, people begged to teach.

Growth caused new problems. Three times they moved to larger meeting halls, and every time, they lost a few members. They first rented a hall for seven days each week. When they outgrew the facility two years later, they found a neighborhood school, which they met in for about two years. It didn't work as well as the hall, because the school wanted the church to pay for all the maintenance, and the school wasn't always available.

Latin Americans, steeped in Catholicism, do not consider a church real unless it has a building. To acquire a building, the church began meeting in members' homes and saving the rental money. Earlier, in the 1960's, churches of Christ had purchased a building for radio outreach. When the radio program ceased, another group met there for a while. When they abandoned it, the Lapa church moved in. The building was located in the neighborhood of Butanta, west and a little south of Lapa. The Landon's bought a van and used it to transport the members from Lapa. As it turned out, many of the members lived closer to Butanta anyway.

Brazilian society is based on a patron-client relationship. When one needs a job, help in educating his children, and many other necessities of life, one goes to the patron. The patron uses his contacts to assist the client in obtaining what is needed. Where a person works, what he does for a living, where he lives, and even his set of friends depend on whom he knows rather than what he knows. The entire society operates in this mode. A person may be a patron to one and a client to another.

This cultural thought pattern impacts leadership in the church. The term they use to describe the patron-client relationship is "ignejinha," which literally means "little church." Churches that adopted that model grew. The concept of having a plurality of elders leading the church creates problems, because it is so foreign to their life-style. They expect the church to have a "responsava," or responsible one, as the leader no matter if he is a preacher or an elder. This works fine for church plants as people naturally consider the evangelist as the leader. As the church matures, the attitude may destroy the church.

Brazilians believe that a person just can't help sinning. That's why Latin culture places many restrictions on a single man and a single woman. If left alone, they just won't be able to help themselves. This feeling of helplessness against sexual sin carries across all sins. Michael spent much time teaching James 1.

Americans and Brazilians differ in direct versus indirect speech and have varying attitudes toward relationship versus productivity. They say what they think you want to hear. Michael related the time when he placed an order for stationary. When the order was due, he called and asked, "Is the stationary ready?" The man answered, "No, it will be ready tomorrow." The next day he went to the store to pick it up, but the clerk said, "No, it's not ready. We need you to look at this." When Michael first called, the clerk said what he thought Michael wanted to hear. But when he went by, he accidentally did what the clerk really wanted. The clerk felt a need for direct relationship at the expense of productivity. But Brazilians can't just say, "We need you to come." This culture of indirect speech carried into church activities where people dropped hints and expected Michael to interpret them. Michael tried to convince them to speak openly at church, and some did. However, speaking openly can be construed as rude. They overlook directness from Americans, but have difficulty accepting it from other

Brazilians. They would say things about Michael like, "He steps on my toes, but still, he helps me."

Collective units and family are critical to Brazilians. Families are the most important. When they attend a private university, every student in a major takes exactly the same courses in exactly the same order. They have the same classmates all the way through the university, and this forms a strong unit. Michael, as we do in the U.S.A., taught that members should grow individually. After listening to him for about eighteen months, a woman asked him what he meant by growing individually. He said, "Reading your bible at home and praying individually." Her face clouded and she said, "You mean we can do things at home by ourselves." To her and many others, any important spiritual or physical activity required group participation.

Yet, Michael often heard Brazilians talk about being individualistic. He related this story to illustrate their individualistic-collective unit view. Two men lived in a high crime area and went to all their neighbors seeking an agreement from thirty-one of them to contribute enough money to pay a guard one day per month. When they had all thirty-one signed up, they hired the guard. At end of month, only fifteen families paid. The two men convinced the guard to work another month hoping more neighbors would pay. At end of the second month, only seven paid. After asking why, the two men found that several of the families that never paid anything bragged about how they took advantage of the ones who paid. In Portuguese, this is called "tirar advantagem." Brazilians define the family as the individual. It's permissible to cheat someone who is not your own family, but it's disgraceful to cheat a family member.

Michael taught the new Christians to consider the church as family, because all are brothers and sisters through the blood of Jesus. The church then provided the unit where important things could be done. Unlike in the United States, the Sao Paulo Christians spent almost every holiday together because the church was their family. Because they adopted the family concept, they usually shared more of their earthly goods with each other than do Americans. Sometimes, members formed closed groups, excluding some. That happened after the Landons left.

A male is not a man in Brazil until he is married and has a family. Michael met that definition when the church was planted in Lapa. A never-married man could have difficulty being accepted as a leader.

The Landons used their family to teach the Brazilians about child discipline. Most Brazilians don't believe a child can learn anything until it is at least four years old. Thus, they don't discipline their children. Susan set up bible classes and taught the children, demonstrating through action and disciplining their own children that the children were very capable of learning. She taught other women how to teach.

For six and a half of their eight years in Sao Paulo, people lived with the Landons. Most were Brazilians trying to get a new start. Tears rise in Michael's eyes and his voice wavers when he tells about how those people said living with him and Susan changed their lives. He also said that when they left, the people were more attached to Susan than to him because she modeled how to live while he was more the intellectual guy.

Time and punctuality doesn't have the same importance as in the U.S.A., partly due to lack of control. When one must ride the unreliable public transportation to go anywhere, there is no way to control arrival times.

Social relationships are important, and Brazilians love getting together. An invitation to Sunday dinner means a longer commitment than it does in the United States. Typically, worship and the ensuing fellowship time ended at about 12:45. It might take forty-five minutes to an hour to get to the couple's home. The hostess never began dinner preparation until the guests arrived, so the meal would be served around 3:00 or 3:30. It is extremely rude to eat and run. The host and hostess expect to talk and visit, so one can't graciously leave until around 7:00 or 8:00. Michael sometimes found this hard when he was tired and wanted to crash at home.

Michael's hometown congregation fully supported them. He sent them monthly reports that included what he did, bible studies in progress, and where he spent the working fund. He always included statistics on Sunday morning attendance. By including data on attendance that month, last month, and a year previously, he was able to demonstrate growth. He found that making charts of this same data and posting them in Lapa assembly area instilled an expectation of growth among the members. He posted charts of average attendance in six months segments. The only time the bars shortened was when growth forced a move to a new and larger meeting place.

The Landons planned to furlough to the States every two years, but visa problems forced them to delay their first visit for an additional eighteen months. Thereafter, they returned approximately every two years except when Susan returned to visit her severely ill mother. During the furloughs, they spent the first month at the supporting congregation making slide presentations, visiting teen and adult classes, and fellowshipping with members. The second month was reserved for family visitation.

During the furloughs, Michael noticed that he wanted to sleep much of the time. Only later during his doctorate studies did he learn why. Living in large cities and being constantly on the go produces stress that activates one's adrenaline glands. He had become addicted to his own adrenaline. When life slowed down, the adrenaline producing glands also slowed and his energy level dropped.

On his last furlough, his supporting eldership surprised him by announcing that they were terminating his support. They said it was not because of his work ethnic, doctrine, or results, but was due to his not encouraging them to send campaigns to Lapa-Butanta. Because the supporting congregation had asked Michael to spend six to twelve months raising funds for a new building, the Landons had stored all their household effects in Sao Paulo. The elders gave him six months to find support elsewhere. Michael also understood that they committed to supplying funds for them to set up a new household since their goods were in San

Paulo. Michael and Susan wanted to return to Brazil and tried to raise money from other congregations. The timing was terrible as the Berlin Wall had just fallen and most churches were looking toward Eastern Europe. Michael found a secular job, but when he lost it, they moved to Michigan where he worked as a chemist and studied to obtain a doctorate in ministry. His hometown church did fly Susan to Sao Paulo to ship their household goods eighteen months later.

The elders did not honor the agreement to set up a new household, and the Landons found themselves burdened with a large monthly payment and little or no income. When Michael asked one elder about the household fund, the man responded, "Michael, you knew this sort of thing happens to missionaries when you became one." According to Michael, this congregation has a long history of firing missionaries and local preachers.

Michael's not being able to return shocked the Brazilian Christians. Prior to his departure, the local church paid all their utilities and supported a part-time minister. They had no building payments. Since the Landons left, the church has not had a full-time evangelist.

The patron-client culture soon impacted the church. About half of its members were born and raised in Sao Paulo and about half had been born elsewhere and transferred there because of work. While Michael was there, both groups trusted him and looked to him as the leader. Another man had unsuccessfully sought the patron role, and after the Landons could not return, acquired it. Sadly, the man didn't consider himself to be the patron of all, only those born in Sao Paulo. He systematically ran the others off. Some of the Sao Paulo born Christians saw what he was doing and also left. Church attendance, which had grown from six to ninety, fell to only the man's family. Finally, he moved away and some of those who had left began to assemble in the building again. Today, about forty adults regularly meet to worship God.

Based on recommendations from other missionaries, Michael did most of the preaching. Earlier missionaries had trained Brazilians to preach, and then said, "Preach, we're going to sit in the pew and watch you." The first generation Brazilian preachers accepted this model, so they trained younger men and then sat in the pew and watched. Michael wanted to demonstrate that leaders lead rather than becoming office managers.

He determined to work a minimum of two nights per week but not more than three. He did not want to neglect his family. This practice allowed him to say to people who brought friends who wanted to study, "Great, you teach him." As the men learned, Michael appointed men to direct the various church ministries.

They followed the American pattern of men's business meetings overseeing the church in the absence of elders. Always, the Brazilian pattern of patron-client underplayed the men's meetings. When the patron learned Michael wasn't returning, he abolished all ministry leaders and concentrated power in himself.

Campaigns played an important role in Michael's life. He had been on six campaigns to San Palo and written his master's thesis about campaigns at Oklahoma Christian University. His first campaign was a wonderful experience, and he, as well as, most other campaigners returned changed for life. The second was also really great, but on the third, he noticed a pattern. The efforts weren't really designed to be evangelistic, just to raise emotions. Some of the congregations sought campaigns from desperation. They thought a campaign would make everything better, but if a church is not evangelistic and open, the campaign won't make them so. Michael emphasized that campaigns that encourage the local church and give it an emotional shot in arm are important. He only objects when emotional lifts are the only result.

Campaigns impact small cities more than large ones because they become the talk of the town and garner lots of attention. When people come, they can be more evangelistic. In large cities, they often go relatively unnoticed.

Campaigns didn't fit Michael's strategy in San Palo as they always emphasized foreignness. Every year, the pulpit minister from his supporting congregation brought a team of college students. They couldn't understand why Michael didn't want them to come where he worked, which probably created anger along with confusion. Most missionaries view campaign groups with mixed feelings. Although they can be helpful, they can burden the missionary with more follow-ups than he can effectively manage. However, most missionaries bow to their supporter's desires. Michael says he would too, if he had it to do over. He emphasized that he is not anti-campaign, and in fact, led one last year. He wants people to lead them because they get results, not because they make the campaigners feel good.

Michael says campaigns can be very beneficial. Even if they don't provide conversions, they can supply new contacts. New contacts require adequate post-campaign resources. Working churches get tired and need a shot in arm; campaigns can be wonderful for them. Early Brazilian campaigns encouraged congregational singing. Brazilians didn't know how to sing, and campaign groups taught them. Now native Brazilians enjoy singing in the American pattern of four-part harmony. The greatest benefit of a campaign is the change in the campaigners. All come back excited, and this is the best way to recruit new missionaries. All the missionaries that have recently gone to Sao Paulo had first gone on a campaign.

The Landons sudden loss of support while on furlough intensified their reverse culture shock. They had no home, no household goods, and an uncertain future. They had adapted to the Brazilian lifestyle and loved the music and food. Relationships were high on their priority and productivity took second place. The very things that had been problems at first were now incorporated into their lifestyle. When Americans invited them into their home for dinner, they would arrive at 5:30 as asked and visit until 10:00. At least half of those who invited them had something else scheduled later in the evening. The host would slip around and call to cancel the other plans. The Landons had learned in Brazil to stay after dinner and visit.

Michael laughs about an experience he had in his native country after three years living immersed in Brazilian culture and language. While in the States, he dropped by to pick up some pictures that had been developed. He handed the young lady a check and she asked, "Is everything on the front OK?" He thought, "Front of what?" She began waiting on another customer while he searched for her meaning. He checked his clothes and even went outside to see if a sale sign was on the door. When she returned, she was looking at the check and realization dawned that she wanted to know about the address. Relieved, he said, "Yes, it's alright." But then she said, "I need your license." License sounds a lot like the Brazilian word for permission. He thought, "permission to do what?" She returned to the other customer while again he sought the answer. Then he thought, "She wants my identification. But, I don't have an identification card here. What do they call that card that gives permission to drive?" Finally, he asked, "Do you need my car license?" She said, "driver's license." He felt foolish, and as he walked away, he grabbed the counter. What an unstable world!

Michael's face brightened as he thought about the rewards he and his family received by living and working in Brazil. "Seeing the fruits of our labor in peoples' lives is primary," he said. "We cheered when they converted, watched as they matured in Christ, and rejoiced with them as they brought their friends. Sometimes, although the Lord is working in our lives, results aren't dramatic. In Brazil, they were dramatic. We witnessed divorce actions stopped and strong marriages develop. We saw people eager to teach and studying diligently to prepare themselves to teach."

He said they grew more in Brazil than they would have in the United States. Not only did they learn to live and adapt in another rich culture, they learned to interpret the bible better. Brazilians ask questions that Americans never think about. Their questions impacted how he read the bible and taught. He had always believed the bible was true, but now it became real. He saw real people and real social situations in the bible that in many ways are similar to ours. It demonstrated how God acted then and how he could be active now. Realization that God is active has changed his life. When one moves to a new culture, support groups and props disappear, and he must ask if God will provide support. He found the answer is, "Yes, he will."

One day while in Brazil, a church member called and said Michael needed to cast a demon out of his relative. Michael knew that some day such a call would come and had been studying and praying about demons. He said, "I decided the bible says that the Holy Spirit inhabits me, so it doesn't matter what the person's problem is, medical, psychological, or even a real evil spirit. I don't have to be afraid of it because the Holy Spirit is with me. I could encounter the person without fear no matter what happened. That was a defining moment in my life"

He maintains confidence that God works in his life. During the thirty months he worked on his doctorate in Michigan, money was always short. Every month when he prepared the budget, expenses always exceeded income by more than $300. Yet, they never paid a bill late. Somehow, they always had just enough. He said, "That is God's power at work." He laughed and said, "We also never had any extra. When I would get a bonus, within two weeks our old car would break down and the repair bill was always within $20 of what I received."

Michael believes living in Brazil favorably impacted his children's character. His youngest son remembers the six times they were robbed, the pollution and the noise in the city while forgetting many of the good experiences. They were all born in Brazil and considered Sao Paulo their home when they moved to the U.S.A. Michael quoted a statistic that he read several times and would like to find the source. It deals with how many families it takes to raise one person who becomes famous enough to be recognized in Who's Who. As he remembered, it requires 13,000 Baptist ministers, 9,000 Presbyterian ministers, 7,000 dentists, and 3,000 medical doctors, but only 7 missionaries. There are an amazing number of famous people who grew up in a mission field.

Poverty became a major issue for Michael while in Brazil. He wanted to better understand it and studied poverty in a Catholic seminary. His face-to-face contact with it changed his life, and his doctoral dissertation deals with the poverty problem.

After completing his studies, Michael preached in Louisiana for three and a half years and wrote his dissertation. Then he preached in Kansas for two years before moving to Terrell, Texas to teach Religious Studies at Southwestern Christian College. He had been there three years at the time of the interview.

Some Suggested Reading

Annotated Bibliography in J. of Applied Missiology, April 1995 by ACU. This can be viewed at http://www.bible.acu.edu/missions/page.asp? ID=272 and deals with items future missionaries to Brazil should know.

What A Missionary Has A Right To Expect From His Sponsoring Church, by Edward Short. This can be viewed at http://cbti.faithsite.com/content.asp?CID=7088.

Thought Provokers

1. What should be the primary purpose of a campaign to a foreign city? How can one insure the objectives will be met?
2. Name at least three cultural practices that a new missionary to Latin Americans should be aware of.
3. What are the primary rewards of mission work?

Chapter Eleven

Santiago, Chile

Based on an interview with Jeff Hatcher

*W*hen he received an invitation to participate in the University of Colorado's summer program for gifted high school students, Jeff never realized how his life would change. For a soon-to-be Senior, it was heady stuff. As a part of getting acquainted, the graduate students invited the summer students to mountain retreats. The graduate students liked to drink copiously and smoke marijuana, and they encouraged the high schoolers to join them. Jeff realized that continuing to do those sorts of things would kill him. The activities seemed so futile, and as Ecclesiastes says, all vanity. Not a religious person or affiliated with any church at that time, Jeff prayed his first prayer ever, "God, please show me who you are."

After he returned home to Houston, a friend invited Jeff to a high school retreat hosted by a church of Christ. Jeff wondered if God could be answering his prayer. At the retreat, the minister gave him a bible and invited him to read it. He did, and began attending worship and classes. Soon, he put on his Lord in baptism. Jeff says, "When I came out of the water, I was so elated, I wanted to tell whoever would listen about Jesus Christ. I've been excited ever since."

The next year, he enrolled at Texas A&M University and got involved with the A&M church. At age 19 and a sophomore, he went on a trip designated Aggies for Christ in the Orient. They visited several churches and missionaries in Southeast Asia, and then he stayed for a longer period in Baguio City, Philippines. There, he worked with the local church doing evangelistic efforts. Teaching others really turned him on to mission work. Returning to A&M, he changed his major to food science with the idea that everyone had to eat and his major could be useful in taking God's word to developing nations. When he completed the course, he received an invitation to do graduate work in Toxicology. Before he earned the Doctor of Philosophy degree, he did short term work in Mexico, Venezuela, and the Philippines. Mission work was ever on his mind and he wanted to use his training to further that goal.

When he completed his graduate work, he had not found the opportunity to go overseas with a mission team. He went to work for the state of Texas and stayed in College Station where he worked with the singles ministry. One day, Bob Davidson, the A&M church campus ministry called him and said, "Jeff, you should come to this dinner. There's going to be folks there trying to get Aggies to go do mission work." Jeff went. Men from Continents of Great Cities presented a need for a team to go to Santiago, Chile. They presented a specific goal for the work and a plan to reach that goal. "Who could ask for more," he said, "than going with a group of people he would probably love and respect because they were Aggies that wanted to do mission work."

The Santiago team consisted of four couples and three singles. The married couples were Kelly and Julie Grant, Scott and Holly Emery, Mark and Denise Dean, Keith and Michelle Kilmer. Jeff and two single women, Elizabeth Riley and Jill Grove completed the team. They committed to go in 1997, came together in 1998, and went in March 1999.

Eight congregations with an average membership of about 30 had previously been planted in Chile's capitol city. They were concentrated in the southern part of the city and close together, because the previous missionary teams had worked with the poorer class of people. A few congregations had come into being as a result of church splits, and they didn't fellowship with some others.

Jeff's team targeted planting a church among the middle class who lived nearer downtown Santiago. Since the city had a population of about 6.5 million, the need was clear.

They envisioned a church that would be easily accessible from any part of town using either public or private transportation.

The team decided to dedicate the first year to language learning, culture adaptation, and city familiarization so they could decide where to plant the church. They moved into middle class suburbs and began immersion language training. This involved living with Chilean families the first month and having to speak the language to survive. Jeff feels very comfortable with the Spanish language now and says that sometimes he has difficulty recalling the English word because the Spanish one jumps in his mind first. He tries not to use Spanish sentence structure while speaking English.

God may have been leading them in this approach, because they met people and developed several contacts during the first year. When they opened the doors for the first worship, about 130 adult Chileans came. All of the visitors came as result of personal contact as no advertisements had been used.

Jeff says they learned that the best outreach is through friends and one-on-one personal contact. The converts includes several teachers and fellow students from the language school. Jeff feels the Chileans are looking for something beyond Catholicism. Approximately 120 Chileans attend Sunday morning classes and worship and about 80% of those participate in small group bible study on Wednesday nights. Growth now comes more through member outreach.

The growth has forced the congregation to go to two worship assemblies, as the former warehouse they now meet in will accommodate about 90 comfortably. They are in the process of purchasing the first property the congregation will own. Finances are coming from the Chilean brethren as well as foundations and supporting congregations in the U.S.A. Each missionary family has a different sponsoring congregation that is committed to the work. The purchased property had been a car dealership and includes a small house. One of their members, an architect, is helping with the demolition and construction plans. Their objective is to build a building that will seat between 300 to 500 people.

Jeff's team responsibility includes leading the benevolence and singles ministries. The singles group includes anyone who doesn't have a spouse and ages range between 20 and 60. Since singles are more receptive to the gospel, the group makes up about half of the congregation.

Divorce is not legal in Chile. When the partners decide the marriage isn't going to work, they separate. If it is agreeable to both parties, they go to the Catholic Church asking for an annulment. This forces them to claim, often falsely, that something was wrong on their application for a marriage license, such as a wrong address. Infidelity is tacitly accepted in the upper middle class, perhaps encouraged by the ban on divorce. In Chilean culture, it is widely accepted among the rich that men will have a mistress. The separation rate of married couples may be a little less than in the U.S., as Chileans do not readily accept divorce.

Culturally, the relationship between men and women is very different. Women in U.S.A. receive more respect and have more rights. The prevailing Chilean view that the woman's job is at home promotes discrimination both professionally and culturally. Some men regard their wives as their property. These feelings have generated a culture that requires more formalities between men and women. The men show formal and overt respect to women as the weaker species rather than respect for her as a person. She is the boss of home and family, although the man thinks her purpose in life is to bear children, keep the house clean, and cook for him.

Jeff found, that being single, he had to observe some rules he never thought existed. He dated some and says he made plenty of mistakes, because he assumed dates would be the same as in U.S.A. They weren't. When he showed what he thought was respect and Godly love, the young ladies thought he was romantically interested. His parents had raised him to be gentle and courteous to everyone, but some misinterpreted it. Eventually, he learned not to be as affectionate at church as he normally would to avoid creating misunderstandings. Most activities involving singles are in groups with lots of other people. If a man and woman go on a date alone, the woman thinks he is very, very serious.

Chileans have a lot more respect for age than do Americans. Jeff has more gray hairs than his other team members, and some members place more import on his statements. He must be careful what he says.

Chilean women respond to the gospel easier than men. The men often look at religion as something that needs to be done, but expect the women to take care of it for the whole family. The team men put themselves into the lives of other men though racquetball, soccer, teaching them English, going to listen to music, and other activities. To be effective, they must take the gospel beyond church walls and outside the context of church. They do this to teach that a relationship with God and between each other goes beyond what men usually regard as "religion."

Their teaching program begins with a set of seven studies designed to introduce the student to the bible, Jesus, and the church. Where they actually begin the lessons depends on the religious background of the student. They supplement these lessons with quarterly seminars designed to encourage Christian growth. Growth is illustrated by a soccer field divided into 4 parts showing development from becoming a member of the church to growing in Christ to taking on responsibility within the church, and to assuming the evangelistic mission of the church. In the U.S.A. some use a baseball diamond and show advancement from base to base. Each missionary tags two or three individuals to mentor. The mentors spend a lot of time with the new Christians, walking with them to teach them service and how to grow up in Christ.

The team's objective is to work themselves out of a job, and prepare the new congregation to go plant another church somewhere else. Initially, Continent of Great Cities told them that other teams using similar strategies required between 10 and 15 years to appoint elders. That's their end goal; to grow the congregation to where they have elders and deacons who want to plant another congregation. Leaders are developing. Some Chileans now lead singing, preach, and reach out in evangelistic studies. The introductory series of 7 lessons were designed so that the teacher could bring along someone else to study along with the student. When a person accepts Christ, he or she is invited to be a part of another study with the idea of training to teach the studies. Progress in transferring teaching roles was illustrated by an event this past fall when Eduardo, a native Chilean, baptized Jennifer, a lady from Michigan who had been visiting for about 18 months.

Before the team went to Chile, they set up a furlough schedule so each member could return to the U.S.A. for two months every two years. They selected two years because other teams had found that if people returned after one year, they were just coming out of the pits of culture shock and getting adjusted to the new life and language. Then, when they returned to their home, everything seemed wonderful, as there were lots of material things to enjoy along with a loving family and friends. They often found it more difficult to return to the mission field as dedicated long-term missionaries.

Jeff thought he would be immune from cultural shock as he had been on several short-term mission efforts. He was well traveled and had seen others experience it. Now, he says that idea was self-delusional. The culture hit him hard after being there a few months. Being single in a strange land disoriented him. The entire team experienced culture shock, and it put stressors on their relationships. The team encouraged one another, as when one was down, another would be up. During their first year, they asked Jerry Hiedrich who was doing mission work in Brazil to come help them get beyond those stressed relationships so they would be prepared for their tasks. Getting through cultural shock before starting the work was beneficial, as the new converts didn't see the strained relationships. When they were ready to open the doors and get started, they had emerged from the depths and were operating on level ground. They could present themselves publicly while earnestly supporting each other.

When he returned on his first furlough, reverse culture shock slammed him. Jeff was amazed at how he viewed American society. When he drove around Houston or went to the Galleria shopping mall, everyone seemed rich. He began to resent them and what he deemed their decadent lifestyle. Then a friend reminded him that he was able to do mission work because these people had money and were giving it to further God's kingdom. That brought him back to reality. "America's definition of poverty can be out of sync with the rest of the world," he said. "It's not what you have; it's what you do with it that is important." When he came back for his second furlough, everything was all right.

The team made an exception to their furlough policy for Jeff after he returned from his normal January furlough with the news that he was going to get married the following August. He and Penne Patterson had met at A&M while both were students. Although they dated some, it wasn't serious. They had kept in contact through the years, while Penne moved to Dallas and worked her way to the position of vice president of a software company. They met again while Jeff interned at Saturn Road Church of Christ in Garland, Texas before going to Chile. One Sunday, he visited the Prestoncrest Church of Christ singles class and there was Penne. He conducted a long distance courtship, and when he returned on his second furlough, she accepted his proposal. Knowing they should not embark on this lifetime commitment without spending more time together, he asked the team for permission to come back in June before their August wedding. They granted it and the Saturn Road congregation put him to work with the Hispanic ministry, teaching bible classes, and encouraging the church in missions. They allowed him to continue this arrangement for five months after the wedding so he and Penne could start their marriage adjustments in familiar surroundings rather than quickly moving to Chile. The team warned him to be prepared to meet culture shock again as he had been out of Chile for seven months. He is determined to ease Penne's encounter, as she will also enter the immersion language school. They returned December 29, 2003, a day after the interview.

When asked about his major accomplishments in the last five years, Jeff listed the establishment of a strong base for a middle class church. He feels the wonderful group of singles will serve to spur the congregation on to love and good works. The Chileans are learning service and leadership. Several song leaders and bible study leaders have come through the singles group.

He hopes singles won't be such a large part of the congregation in the future. In 2004, the team will emphasize family outreach though marriage enrichment seminars. They hope to bring in entire family units and look for leaders within those units. They follow Paul's instructions to Timothy by teaching those who can teach others. They are thrilled at the visible fruit of their efforts.

Jeff has a few things he would like anyone beginning mission work in Chile to know. First, missionaries should be sensitive to the relationships between men and women. Learn the required formalities and don't communicate unintended messages.

Second, if the goal is to bring people to Christ, ask God to bring someone to you. He will! Keep your eyes open for the person. God may bring the waiter or waitress, your next-door neighbor, the mail carrier, or the grocer. Remember, you are the aroma of Christ to all you meet. If you are seeking the lost, you will have the fragrance of life. Contacts may come 24/7. God has put you there for a reason, be alert to the opportunities he puts in your path. Jeff says he is confident that he missed some he could have taught if his eyes had been open.

Jeff emphasizes that one should not be afraid of being who you are. "Some put too much pressure on themselves to fit into the culture," he said. "The facts are, if you are from the U.S.A., you will always be from the U.S.A., you will always be a Gringo to the Chileans. Accept it, and love the people at all times. Love transcends all cultural boundaries and nothing can withstand its force. Loving relationships have been the basis for bringing people to Christ.

"When one realizes that the awesome responsibility of spreading the aroma of Christ is ever present, it becomes easy to speak to others about Christ." The joy of telling others and seeing the happiness that Christ brings into their lives is what keeps Jeff going.

When Jeff first went to Santiago, he planned to be there as long as it took for the new congregation to become self-sustaining and reproductive. As a couple, the picture has changed. Jeff and Penne have committed to spend at least the next three years working there. They will be looking for God to provide some answers concerning their family and their effectiveness.

Thought Provokers
1. When a church commits to plant a new church in a different culture, how long should it commit to provide support?
2. Why did Jeff refer to "aroma" when describing evangelism?
3. What is the most powerful weapon we have to break down cultural barriers? How should we use it?

Chapter Twelve

Single and Alone

Based on an interview with Chris Nichol

$\mathcal{C}$hris Nichol listened intently to the antidotes of Larry Moran, a former missionary to Venezuela. Moran, an evangelist in Edmonton, Alberta Canada, was assigned to disciple Chris, an intern in the Edmonton School of Evangelism. Even before enrolling in the school, Chris had dreamed of working in a foreign country, learning a new language, and perhaps marrying a foreigner. Now, as he listened to Moran, he became excited at the prospects of preaching God's message in a foreign country. As he continued to study the audio tapes from Sunset International Bible Institute and work alongside the Edmonton evangelists, he longed for a missionary opportunity.

When Herb Anderson, one of the Edmonton evangelists and an elder, returned from his annual trip south of the Canadian border with the news that a Texas church was looking for a man to go to Lithuania, Chris lost no time in applying.

After a three-month stay at the Waterview Church of Christ in Richardson, Texas, Chris moved to Vilnius, the capitol city of Lithuania, on January 4, 1997. Chris was single and barely 23 years old. Keith and Norma Levy who had served several times as short-term workers in Vilnius accompanied him. The supporting church planned to send short-term workers each month to assist Chris. They did for a few months, and then no more short-term workers went.

Almost two years earlier in May 1995, Waterview members planted the church in Vilnius though a campaign held in the Hotel Lituva. During the campaign, about 170 people came to study the bible. They came from a variety of cities and villages throughout the country, and most were World Bible School or World English Institute students. Many came more for English than the Bible, but several became very interested in learning more of God's word. During the campaign, the group rented a flat in downtown Vilnius and determined to staff it with short-term workers until a full time missionary arrived. Throughout the next two years, short-term workers volunteered to teach daily bible classes at the study center and preach on Sundays. Each worker team stayed for a month. A couple moved in October 1995 with the intention of staying five years, but due to circumstances, they only stayed three months.

When Chris arrived in January 1997, several members had fallen away, disenchanted because a full time worker had not arrived sooner. From the beginning, the people, newly freed from Communistic rule, had difficultly believing the church was there to stay. Satan used the lack of a full time worker to fuel their disillusionment. Chris started to rebuild the church. His goals were to teach as many as possible, teach them to teach, and to develop leaders.

A rented flat in prestigious Old Town served as study center and worship facilities. Many World Bible School and World English Institute students came to study and brought friends. The church began to grow. Construction near the Bible study center and attendance growth made it desirable to look for new and larger facilities. Since all of the members and students depended on public transportation, they located the new study and worship center near the central bus station and train depot.

Chris conducted most of his teaching as either one-on-one or in small groups. He used a variety of techniques, many of which he had learned in Edmonton during his conversion and internship. Waterview also supplied video material developed by Robert Oglesby, *The Story,* which was translated into Russian and Lithuanian. Chris dedicated the first study session to learn the student's religious background and to create a bond. Many of the students had no religious background, and few possessed even a rudimentary Bible knowledge. Most of the time, he was faced with either establishing a belief in God or convincing the person of the authority of God and the bible. Several former atheists learned to love and trust Jesus.

At first, Chris taught through translators. The language problem was compounded in Vilnius. Not everyone Chris taught could speak Lithuanian as the population included both Lithuanian and Russian speakers. During the Soviet occupation, everyone spoke Russian. After liberation, many Lithuanians refused to speak Russian although they were fluent. Older Russians could not speak Lithuanian, which is an old, difficult language based on an alphabet similar to English. But Lithuania was home for these ethic Russians, many of whom had never lived anywhere else. Younger people could speak both languages. Teaching through translators brought several of the translators to Christ.

Chris and his supporting congregation decided that the language in the church needed to be Lithuanian as that was the national language. He immediately initiated language study using private tutors. Later, Chris enrolled in the University of Vilnius, where he became fluent in the language.

Worship and public bible study was translated into both Lithuanian and Russian. Chris preached in English and a stand-up interpreter translated into Lithuanian. A tour guide transmitter and headsets were purchased to permit a Russian translator to whisper her translation as the other person translated into Lithuania. Songs were sung in all three languages.

Tensions between Russian and Lithuanians were often high in society. Before liberation, Russians were favored, but the roles were reversed after Lithuanians came into power. Many Russians were forced from their jobs because they could not speak Lithuanian. In church, most people were able to put their prejudices aside, however, some older members whose families had lost land and people would not. Sadly, many stopped attending worship.

Today, Lithuanian is the primary language used in public assemblies and the headsets are still used for Russian only speakers. They also provide visiting English speakers means of participating.

Being single had some benefits, Chris remembers. His schedule could be more flexible than a married man; he had more time available for work, and didn't have to help a wife adjust to a new culture. At the same time, he faced waves of severe loneliness with no one to understand and lift him up.

Chris had difficulty knowing whether some of the single women were more interested in him as a future spouse or in learning about God. During the Soviet occupation, many men turned to alcohol to cover their frustrations. Boys were prone to follow in their fathers' footsteps. Christian girls found few boys they wanted to date. They found kind and godly Chris very attractive. He refused to date for the first year he was there. Chris is pleased that several of the women he dated are still faithful. He and his wife Viktorija began dating after he had been in country over five years. They married in March 2003.

Chris said, "Most of the time I looked at living in the new culture as an adventure, which helped a lot. Since I was single, I had no choice but to rely upon Lithuanians for friendship and support, which eased the impact of culture shock. There were many times when I looked at the Lithuanian culture with disdain, but those times usually passed quickly. Now, with a Lithuanian wife, I am completely immersed into the local culture, and understand it quite well.

"The biggest cultural difference was perhaps the general attitude towards life, future, and religion. Since Lithuania was under Soviet rule for 50 years, the way people looked at each other, at their country, and at their future, was and is very different than attitudes I had known in Canada. I found Lithuanians to be pessimistic about their country and future, about their relations with others, and very mistrusting."

Asked about his first impressions of Lithuania, Chris said, "I was really excited about being in the forbidden lands of the former Soviet Union, so I looked at everything with adventure and interest. The people were very friendly, and I enjoyed visiting in their homes and talking about their lives and history. Life was simple, and people had a much simpler lifestyle than I had in Canada. The first few months especially taught me a lot about what "simple" means. And that simple was better."

Chris continued, "Simple meant, a person or lifestyle that wasn't complicated, or filled with a lot of ambition. People often use the term to describe a person in a positive way, and not in a negative way like in Canada. I had thought of simple as being someone or something that wasn't very bright; whereas people here saw it as something special. A person who did not complicate relationships, or place personal gain above relationships."

Yet there were difficult times. Shopping, instead of being pleasant, often became a traumatic experience. Steeped in Soviet culture, sales people were very rude and impatient. Store clerks acted as if walking into their store made Chris guilty. Security guards watched him as if they expected him to steal. When that happened to him, especially on a cold dark winter evening, he just wanted to go home to his flat and get away from any and all Lithuanians.

When he arrived in 1997, Lithuanians had a hard time trusting others. They had, as was the case in much of the USSR, learned to live double lives. They would speak and act one way in public (or at church), and speak and act very differently at home. Chris said, "At times, I misinterpreted people's actions and intentions and sometimes it lead to misunderstandings and rocky relationships. On some occasions, he felt betrayed by Lithuanians who acted duplicitously and at other times, he offended those he did not understand. Those experiences sometimes caused him to look at Lithuania and its culture in a negative light.

An adventurer at heart, Chris continued to view his role in Lithuania optimistically. There were enough pleasant experiences to overcome the unpleasant ones. Seeing the joy in his students as they accepted Christ as their savior, and watching new Christians make dramatic changes in their lifestyles fueled his desire to overcome the culture shock and continue to work and teach in Lithuania. Gradually, he adapted to the language and the culture until he decided he wanted to continue to live and teach in Lithuania for the foreseeable future.

Scott Heft, who had been on several campaigns to Lithuania, resigned his job in Texas and moved to Vilnius about ten months after Chris arrived. Scott planned to earn his living in Lithuania for a year teaching English. Having another single man with similar goals and values provided Chris companionship and support. They spent as much time together as possible and charged each other with holding themselves accountable for their work and lives.

Scott soon met and fell in love with a Lithuanian lady. After they married, Chris found himself alone again. Scott and Virginija continued to live in Vilnius and they often fellowshipped with Chris, but he had lost his single friend. Still, Chris did not find his life partner for almost four more years.

The church grew slowly at first. Some people, who had accepted Christ before he arrived, fell away. After struggling for two years, Sunday attendance grew by about ten percent in 1999, and then jumped by 48 percent and 101 percent respectively the next two years. It stabilized at about 50 during 2001 and 2002. The growth strained the worship facilities and forced the congregation to search for new quarters. Schools and public auditoriums denied them time due to Catholic influence. They finally found an auditorium in Old Town with a room for children's classes and a stage. They began worshipping there every Sunday morning.

Children Relief Fund proved valuable in helping the church to grow. Christians in North America contributed twenty-five dollars per month, twenty-two of which was provided to the Vilnius church. It was used to assist needy families. Although twenty-two dollars a month doesn't sound like much, it was often more than a third to half of the families' income. CRF had, with experience throughout the world, developed rules. The children had to attend school daily and bible class weekly. Christians would take responsibility for purchasing the food, supplies, or clothing the child needed. The parents did not handle the money, as many were not capable of doing so. Attendance at bible class increased, both children's and adults. Since the parents would not allow their small children to come alone, either they or an older sibling would bring them. They stayed and learned and several became Christians.

The new facility turned out to be depressing as the owners would not permit a sign at the front and the entry into the auditorium was circuitous. Attendance declined and they moved to a well-situated hotel. These moves along with some other difficulties caused average attendance to decrease to 37. The Bible Study Center has moved to a more prominent location. It is smaller as the church no longer meets there for worship. It is located on a well-traveled street and it's bright interior invites people in. Once again the attendance is rising.

In 2000, a young male member enrolled in Sunset International Bible Institute Extension School to study in Vilnius. The Vilnius church supported him so he could quit his job and study full time. Following Edmonton's pattern, Chris created a three-year program combining the SIBI video classes and on-the-job training. Today, Ilia Amosov serves as evangelist and two other men are enrolled as interns. Chris did not want to send anyone out of the country to study for fear they would not come back. Before Chris arrived, a promising young man was granted a full scholarship to a Christian school. Although the scholarship specified that the man would return after completing his degree, he did not.

Weekly men's classes included both bible study and leadership training. Chris involved the men in the church's day-to-day decisions from the beginning. At first, many of the decisions involved benevolent requests. The locals better understood people's needs and resources and made appropriate and loving decisions. As the men matured in Christ, they began to make decisions about many aspects of the work. When questions arose that impacted the entire congregation, meetings were held to discuss the issues.

Soon after he arrived, Chris followed his supporting congregation's guidance to tell the people that he would be there only until they could assume everything themselves. That news discouraged some as they interpreted it to mean that he would be leaving very soon. Several were still disturbed by the short tenure of the previous missionary, and they worried about being abandoned in their new faith. He quit emphasizing his leaving, as permanence was needed.

Never feeling comfortable in the role, Chris began and taught weekly ladies classes. When short-term workers came, he always enlisted the women as teachers. Today, the women conduct their own classes and love to get together for study and fellowship.

Chris kept his sponsoring congregation informed through weekly work reports, monthly financial reports, and yearly visits. On his annual furloughs, he spent two weeks in Texas reporting and visiting in homes and classes. He also received two weeks to return to Canada to visit his family and friends. During his returns, a member of the supporting congregation dedicated a month to teach at the study center and preach. As the local men developed, the need for a short-term worker diminished.

When one of the men who had served as a short time worker organized a summer camp, Chris enthusiastically joined forces. Beginning in 1998 with 55 children, the camps grew to three sessions with 240 children attending. Two camps sessions are organized according to age, one for ages 7-12 years and one for 12-18. The government in Belarus forbids Christian camps, so about 50 children and sponsors travel from Minsk to north Lithuania. The third camp is Russian-speaking and includes children from Minsk and Lithuanian.

Camps provided many of the children their only contact with the church. They impacted many families and have influenced several to put on Christ as Lord. Lithuanians are nominally Roman Catholic and are often suspicious of other religions. The children's experiences at camp have helped many parents discount rumors that the church of Christ is a cult.

At the first camp, the children responded wonderfully to the counselors and activities. The Soviets had built the campgrounds and used them to promote and teach Communism. After liberation, the camps continued, but most had no structure. The children were left to entertain themselves and often, the entertainment was not constructive. The children loved the adult attention shown them, and they loved the bible classes. Some stated, "This is the only happy week of my life." That touched the North Americans and Lithuanians alike.

Camps emphasized Christ and His values. For many children, this was their only experience with a positive male role model. At first, North Americans filled all the counselor positions, but as Lithuanians developed, they filled more counselor roles. Chris states, "Camp has become a primary outreach tool. We organized camper meetings in two cities where no church exists and we are preparing the ground for planting. Several children have first met Christ at camp and their parents have met Him through them. Many Christians have grown through their involvement with these camps and several have put on Christ because of their influence."

Asked what he would do differently, Chris replied, "I wouldn't try to go to a new country or a new city by myself. It is just too difficult. Taking the gospel and planting churches should be a team activity. I think that's why Jesus sent his disciples out in pairs."

At the time of this writing, Chris is planning on returning to Edmonton, Canada in the summer of 2004. Obtaining the necessary immigration papers for his wife is time consuming and problematic as governments move slowly. He will leave the church in Vilnius with two trained evangelists, two interns studying to become evangelists, and many friends.

Thought Provokers
1. What special skills does an evangelist need to move to a foreign culture alone and maintain both staying power and effectiveness?
2. Should mission works be concerned with providing humanitarian aid as well as spiritual food? What are some ways this can be done?
3. What are the pros and cons of a missionary marrying within the culture?

Chapter Thirteen

Klaipeda, Lithuania

Based on an interview with Kevin Carson

A wave of loneliness engulfed Kevin and Catharine as they stood with their three and a half year old son and eighteen month old daughter that cold mid May morning. They bravely waved goodbye at the bus bouncing through a few chug holes while pulling away from Hotel Klaipeda. Less than two weeks earlier, they had arrived on the same bus with a campaign group from Waterview Church of Christ, Richardson, Texas. The twenty-two Christians came to plant the church in Lithuania's primary port city of about 400,000 people. During the previous two years, approximately 800 Lithuanians living in and around Klaipeda had enrolled in World Bible School and World English Institute courses. Several of their teachers had come on the campaign. During the two weeks, almost a 1000 people came to the hotel to hear Bible lessons and hopefully meet their correspondence course teachers. Lectures and classes had been presented in English and translated into Lithuanian and Russian and twenty-three souls had put on their Lord in baptism.

One of the elders of the supporting congregation told Kevin, "Well, you now have an instant congregation." Then he and nineteen others boarded the bus to return to Texas. The burden of caring for these new Christians weighed heavily on Kevin. He had a list of names, but he wouldn't recognize many of the owners if he met them on the street. Over two hundred people were still active in daily bible study. Fortunately, Herman Alexander and five of his students from the Center for Christian Education arrived to teach for three weeks.

During the previous thirteen days, Kevin had been torn between participating in the campaign and getting his family oriented in a city they had only visited for a few days four months earlier. They moved into a small flat near the building he rented to serve as a study and worship center. The study center would be located in Old Town near the central market. However, it was still under construction and the present campaign site would only be available to them for a few more days. Kevin set out to find an interim location. A music hall was rented for Sunday assemblies and a tailor school for daily bible lessons. He stopped by the classes as much as possible to meet some of the students. Invariably, the teacher would introduce him and tell the students, "We're all going to be gone, but Kevin will be here." He felt inadequate to care for all these precious souls.

Logistics consumed Kevin's time. The Center for Christian Education group spent all their time teaching as that fitted their desires and talents. Kevin attended to record keeping, making sure interpreters were available and paid, guaranteeing the classes had a place to meet, and other myriad minutia. He prepared for the rapidly approaching time when only he and Catharine would be left. Some mornings, he wanted to just lie in bed. But, he knew the tasks wouldn't go away, he just had to roll up his sleeves and get at it. As soon as he got into meeting people and studying with them, all apprehensions disappeared.

Although they had studied Lithuanian language audiotapes before going, they couldn't communicate or understand when Lithuanians rattled off the words. Their inability to communicate was reinforced early in the campaign when they took their children to a park. While their daughter played with a Lithuanian child, Kevin and Catharine smiled and nodded at the other set of parents. Catharine told Kevin to hand a flyer advertising the campaign to the couple. When the woman read the flyer, her face twisted and darkened. After a moment or so, while Kevin and Catharine wondered what they did, she showed it to her husband and motioned for him to talk to them. After some attempts in broken English, he finally drew them a picture. The flyer had been written in English and translated into Lithuania before being printed in Texas to bring to Klaipeda. Somewhere along the line, one letter got omitted. Instead of advertising a study of God's word, the flyer now proclaimed sex studies. Fortunately, the flyers were still in the box. The Carsons could only wonder what other unforeseen landmines lay in wait.

They immediately located a language teacher. Kevin spent much of his time at the study center with native speakers. The people came voluntarily and encouraged his feeble attempts to communicate. He always had a translator to smooth out misunderstandings. Most days, Catharine bundled up the kids in a backpack and stroller and bounced them across the cobblestone streets to the grocery store without a translator. This was a depressing time as the groceries were distributed among several tiny departments within a small, ill-stocked store. Each department positioned their wares behind a counter manned by a stern appearing matron. The shoppers could not pick up anything to look at it, and the labels were unreadable at a distance in the dim light. The way it was supposed to work was that the shopper would ask the clerk to hand them what they wanted. Then, the shopper paid at each department. One would have to stand in line, shop, and pay in each of the different departments for milk, meat, bread, vegetables, and fruit. Having a line of impatient shoppers behind her as she struggled with the language frustrated Catharine. Yet, her concern for the clerks amazed Kevin. She would say, "What do these women have to be happy about? They work for low wages at boring jobs in dismal surroundings. Many of their husbands are alcoholics. They have no future. What they need is Christ." Still, her stress level jumped every time she visited a store. The Carsons worked with their language teacher to learn a simple phrase like, "One quart of milk, please." They would write it down, study it on the way, and rerun it through their mind while standing in line, only to have it come out garbled when they reached the counter.

They began to refer to the grocery stores as "grunt and point" stores.

The Lithuanian language is an old language, and although it uses an alphabet similar to English, it is ranked as one of the most difficult in the world. When Kevin and Catharine began studying at different times, their proficiency increased. He could concentrate more on bible words and she on shopping words. They really began learning the language when they invited friends to dinner without a translator. They placed a dictionary on the table and struggled to carry on a conversation. The guests could struggle in English if they desired while the Carsons strove to speak the language of the country. Of course, the kids quickly learned several words and assisted the dinner table discussions.

The Carsons don't consider themselves fluent in the language. They can carry on conversations and they understand more than they can say. They recognize the words people are saying, maybe not every one, but they understand enough of the context to extract the meaning. The Lithuanians encouraged them and said they were doing well with the language. "You're probably your own worst critic," Kevin said. "The more you learn, the more you know you don't know."

When children are unhappy, parents get stressed. The Carson's first apartment building had a u-shaped courtyard in front where the children gathered to play. Jesse is outgoing and loves to play with others. When he tried to join the children, they could not communicate. Three to five year olds don't understand about different languages, so all the other children considered him strange. Their treatment made him cry, and then the Lithuanian children would wonder why he was crying. It only made things worse. Kevin wondered, "What have I done to my children?"

Stress jumped big time when Jesse entered kindergarten. The first two days went fine. But then fear set in, and at night, Jesse begged, "Don't make me go to that place." A denominational missionary family had a daughter the same age as Jesse, and after a week, they couldn't stand her crying and stopped taking her. The Carsons believed that learning the skill of facing your fears was important, so they continued to take him to school. They supported him through the first few weeks and Jesse survived and began to thrive. Articles they had read about how missionary kids learned to adapt and gain skills that served them well later in life provided confidence to the parents. Lithuanian became Jesse and Claire's language of play and when they returned to Canada, they continued to play using that language until they met new English speaking friends.

When they got frustrated and felt down, Kevin and Catharine would remember why they had come in the first place. Both were first generation Christians. Kevin had moved to Yellowknife, Canada after graduating high school. While working at a newspaper setting type, he read an ad for a Bible correspondence course from the local Church of Christ. He enrolled and soon became a Christian. When he enrolled in the University of Edmonton, he became involved in the local congregation's evangelistic efforts.

Catharine also enrolled at the University of Edmonton intent on becoming a nurse. One night, a fellow nursing student invited her to a Bible study at the high-rise dormitory. Because of that fellow student's invitation, Catharine became a Christian. She and Kevin met at church and later married. Both remained active in teaching others. Kevin taught drama classes for several years before dedicating himself to full time evangelism.

One of the Edmonton elders returned from a trip to Texas with the news that missionaries were needed to go to Lithuania. He related that more than 800 people studied World Bible School and World English Institute, and there was no one to follow up with them. Chris Nichol, a young man who just completed Edmonton School of Evangelism committed to go to Vilnius, Lithuania, where a church had been planted. Kevin had recently heard Acapella's song *Fallen Walls and Open Doors.* The message that the fall of the Iron Curtain had removed barriers and excuses for not going to Former Soviet Bloc nations impacted his heart. The Carsons decided to go and take the gospel to Klaipeda.

Their enthusiasm and dedication pulled them through the first negative impressions made during an inspection trip to the country. They made the trip in January and snow covered the trees and ground. Even so, everything looked gray, dirty, and run down. Chris, who had only been on site for about two weeks, met them at the dingy airport, got them into an old taxi, and took them to an apartment building. It was an old standard Soviet high-rise apartment building that looked as if no one had ever performed maintenance on it. Walking down the cold, unlighted hallway didn't help. The next morning, they didn't know their address, their phone number, and they had no local money. The children began to get hungry and they had nothing to feed them. Feelings of helplessness and disorientation swept over them. After Chris came with breakfast, the world looked brighter. Two days later, Catharine felt comfortable enough to go for a jog, but lost her bearings. She finally went into a business, but she could only remember the name of one road and it wasn't the one they lived on. She kept saying that name over and over until they understood she was a lost foreigner and got her a taxi. She rode around until she recognized a building. Today, memories of these experiences bring laughter, but at the time they produced disorientation and vulnerability. The bigger picture came into focus when they saw how Chris had been building gospel understanding and a sense of belonging and community among a people who still had difficulty trusting anyone. As they began helping people experience positive Christian fellowship and relationships, a sense of warmth covered all the initial negative experiences and frustrations.

After the first Klaipeda campaign, the Carsons settled into a daily routine of teaching, fellowshipping, and growing the new church. Many of the people who converted during the campaign soon fell away, but those who studied longer before making a commitment followed their new life style. Two groups of teachers came to help during July and August and the congregation grew. Finally, the new study center was completed and the bright, new location demonstrated a sense of permanence. Several months later, the congregation filled the center and a new facility next door was leased. Almost three years later, the growing congregation moved into its own building purchased with a loan from the supporting congregation. At last, the new converts felt the church was there to stay.

By this time, Sunday morning attendance was just under 60. In the next year, it increased to about 75. Two men began an internship to become evangelists. They committed to study the videos produced by Sunset International Bible Institute and to work alongside Kevin for three years. Lithuanian was the language of worship. Kevin worked hard to prepare his sermons and go over them with the church secretary to make sure his grammar and pronunciation were accurate.

Although daily Bible studies continued to be the primary means of bringing people to Christ, other activities influenced outsiders. Summer camps grew from one session per year to two and involved about two hundred children throughout the nation. Four humanitarian aid shipments were distributed to local hospitals, medical clinics, and nursing homes. Rebecca McKinnon, a young woman from Waterview, resigned her secular job and moved to Klaipeda. She worked alongside the Carsons for two years encouraging and teaching young women and girls.

Short time workers from North America spelled the Carsons during their annual month-long furlough. The Carson family looked forward to what the kids called "Back to English." They spent two weeks with the supporting congregation and two weeks with their families in Canada. Although getting a break from the new language was pleasant, furlough time produced some trials. Travel and time changes with children often proved difficult. The love and warmth shown them by the supporting congregation proved positive and they considered it a great part of coming back. They were treated as special guests and people gave copious gifts to them. The gifts produced mixed feelings. Living in a country where people don't have much made them feel uncomfortable to have so much lavished on them. "We didn't want to refuse the gifts," Kevin said, "because people wanted to express their appreciation and love. North America's affluence is far greater than Lithuania's. God has blessed North America and physical blessings can be used for His glory."

"Coming back was kind of like being a kid again," Kevin said. "Staying and eating in different people's homes made us feel like we were imposing although we knew we were welcome and wanted. In Canada, I often had to bum a car and that made me feel like a teen. Not being in full control of our lives made me feel uncomfortable." The children's routine was broken when they ate supper at a different table and slept in different houses. Their minds said, "There are no rules now." They had a lot of fawning grandparents and enjoyed taking advantage of their newfound opportunities.

When asked what he would do differently if he had it to do over again, Kevin said, "I would not want to go with a campaign to start a new work. I would go in first without other workers and get the work started. If I had had a place to live and had gotten family routines set, I would have been more oriented and more involved in the initial work. That would have allowed me to be on top of the needed follow-up."

At first, Kevin and Catharine thought it was a disadvantage not to be a part of a team. They knew the evangelist in Vilnius, but he was two hundred miles away. After they had been in country for a while, they changed their minds. Not being a part of a team forced them to make friends with Lithuanians. If they had had English friends, they might have formed a missionary enclave and associated mostly with them. If they go into another country, they want to go alone.

Kevin said he would have liked to read more about the country before moving, but when they went, there were very few books on Lithuania. They had skills in evangelism, but they lacked appreciation of the difficulties of language acquisition and culture shock. They attended a retreat in Germany after serving for seven months and breathed a big sigh of relief when they learned that what they were experiencing was normal.

"Learning a difficult language before going is just not practical." Kevin said. "You're not in the environment and motivation is lacking. When you're really immersed and must use it to survive is when you learn."

He advises a missionary to locate a cultural mentor as soon as possible. The mentor may help them avoid the cultural mistakes that are sure to arise in a new and foreign country. They laugh now at their cultural faux pas. When they moved into the first study center, they celebrated with a weekend of special gatherings and lessons. Catharine had a dark green and black checked skirt made for the occasion. She wore a white blouse and black scarf with it. On Sunday night, the final night, one woman came up to her and put her hand on Catharine's arm. With a concerned look she asked, "Are you OK?" Catharine said "Sure. Why do you ask?" The woman asked, "Did someone die? We only wear black scarves if we are in mourning." Catharine responded, "Why didn't you tell me Friday instead of Sunday."

Early in the work, the Carsons would be the only ones present on Sunday morning as worship time neared. People would come late, and leave right after worship. Kevin wanted to build a sense of fellowship, as most of the Christians didn't even know each other. Few family units existed, and the new Christians possessed no sense of identity as a body. Potluck dinners worked in North America, and so the Carsons arranged to have some after worship. But in a Catholic culture like Lithuania, people don't take food to the cathedral. They don't set up tables down the middle of aisle and eat. It took a while for the people to accept the new tradition.

Kevin studied with a Russian retired high-ranking army officer. Prior to Lithuania regaining its freedom, over 4000 Russian soldiers were stationed in Klaipeda. Some of them had grown up in Lithuania and considered it home, so when the army left, they stayed. When the officer retired, he lost the prestigious home his family enjoyed and had to move into a small run down apartment. When the Carsons were invited to dinner, Catharine went to market to buy flowers. She knew it was customary to take a gift when going for dinner and knew the people loved fresh flowers. She found a beautiful arrangement and removed the black ribbon, as it didn't look right. Their hosts' eyes widened when they saw the arrangement and didn't even express their appreciation. Unusual behavior! In Russian culture, arrangements of an even number of flowers are reserved for funerals. Everyone, except the Carsons, knew that the arrangement she had purchased was designed for cemeteries and graves.

Kevin said, "You definitely need a good sense of humor to be a missionary."

After being in Klaipeda for four years, the Carsons decided it was time to return to Canada. Several factors played into their decision. They wanted their children to have more time with their Canadian families. They weren't confident of the quality of the Lithuanian schools or the home schooling they were augmenting the local schools with. Their home congregation in Canada had gone through a period of turmoil and needed stability in the pulpit, and asked him to return. They felt the church in Klaipeda had grown well over the years with two local men training to become full time evangelist. Two missionary families from the Edmonton congregation they had confidence in had committed to come. If Kevin stepped out, he felt the locals might step forward and do more. Perhaps they were in his shadow and depended on him too much.

On the day they left Klaipeda, it felt like a funeral. People stood, wearing glum expressions and saying goodbyes with tears running down their cheeks. When the van pulled away and they looked back, the picture of everyone standing there burned in his mind. Several months later, Catharine told Kevin that when they were driving away, she felt they had made a big mistake.

They experienced joy at being back in their home country, seeing their families more often, and being able to preach in English. Yet, Kevin didn't think it right. Lithuania was the frontier of the Kingdom and the need was far greater there. He felt selfish to be back in North America where the church was well established and had multiple generations of Christians to work. There were needs in Edmonton, but the church in Lithuania was still an infant. He didn't find his daily tasks as fulfilling as what he did in Lithuania. Plowing new ground, working with young Christians and teaching them how to pray brought more fulfillment and pleasure. He had been working with the future of the church there.

There was also an economic aspect to his unease. He had gained fulfillment and satisfaction by helping people who barely got by day to day. It seemed wrong to be so comfortable, both physically and spiritually, when he knew he could be making a difference in those people's lives. Things the Carsons thought important didn't seem so important anymore. Although they saw their family more often, they probably saw them for fewer days each year while living in Canada.

The Carsons are returning to Lithuania in a new role, a national resource. They will focus on enabling local leaders to grow rather than doing the work themselves. There are now congregations in three cities. Men and women are teaching classes, making benevolence decisions, and other Christian works. The Carsons will work at their side to assist them in developing skills to keep the Lithuanian congregations strong and evangelistic. The sponsoring church plans that eventually, all North American workers will phase out, and Lithuanians will assume every leadership role. Kevin remembers that when he became a Christian, Edmonton, Canada was a mission site. A Texas congregation supported the preacher. As the church grew, it assumed more and more of his salary and eventually stood on its own. It hired a campus minister and is now training its own evangelists and supplying missionaries. In fact, four of the seven missionary families who worked in Lithuania were from Edmonton. That's the way he sees Lithuanian churches: growing into self-reliance and evangelizing their neighbors.

Thought Provokers

1. What are the pros and cons about missionaries going in teams?

2. What can missionaries and supporting congregations do to help the children to adjust to the new culture and language? How much should the parents try to shield the children?

3. How can a supporting congregation make it easier for the missionary during furloughs?

Chapter Fourteen

Concluding Thoughts

*T*he twelve vignettes in this book represent only a small fraction of each missionary's efforts, accomplishments, and trials. I hope you have been able to glean a few pointers that will be useful in whatever role you play or will play in spreading the Word of God throughout the world. If you haven't meditated on the Thought Provokers provided at the end of chapters Two through Thirteen, I encourage you to do so before reading further.

Those of us who have never lived in a foreign country for several months or years do not appreciate the damaging impact of culture shock to a missionary's attitude or work ethic. Adapting to a new language, different attitudes, unusual shopping patterns, dissimilar entertainment practices, and strange, mystifying cultural norms can sap a person's zeal and dedication. What can we do to help during these times of stress? Communicate concern, understanding, and interest through emails, cards, and letters. Most importantly, pray daily for them and let them know you are praying fervently. All missionaries highly value your prayers.

What can missionaries do to prepare to meet cultural shock? Read about other people's experiences, talk to returned missionaries, and learn as much about the language and culture as you can before going. Should one spend years learning about culture shock? Not according to most missionaries. The most important thing is to go. And when you get there and the shock starts getting to you, share your feelings with the Lord and your fellow Christians. Read the word. Remember why you are there. Don't think it won't happen to you. It will. The severity depends upon your attitude, your personality, and your ability to work through the bad times. Many people get through the shock through seeing the people's joy when they learn about Jesus for the first time. Reliance on God's grace and comfort strengthens one's purpose.

When missionaries return from the field, churches often do not understand or appreciate the reverse culture shock these dedicated workers are undergoing. We just expect them to "suck it up and press on." Every person I interviewed stated that reverse culture shock is harder to deal with than adapting to the foreign culture. One of the most damaging and hard to deal with factors is the stateside Christians' attitude toward them and evangelism. Have we become so cold hearted because we have forgotten the fire that burned within us when we first believed? Have we become like the Laodiceans and are we in danger of being spit from Christ's mouth? I hope not.

Spiritual renewal is a vital consideration for a committed long-term missionary. There are a few places where missionaries can get the associations and training he and she need for their spiritual health. Three, I know of, are Sunset International Bible Institute, Harding University, and Abilene Christian University. In each case, the missionary must bring his own support in order to be able to participate and live for approximately a year. Many cannot take advantage of those resources because supporting congregations don't recognize the value of renewal. If supporters make any financial provisions for returning missionaries, they usually do not exceed three months support. Often, good capable workers leave the mission field instead of returning to plant new churches. Are we wasting valuable and trained resources? My former boss explained why he didn't fire an employee whose mistake had cost the company millions of dollars, "Why fire a person who has learned a valuable lesson and won't make that mistake again?" The people of the world are often wiser than the people of the light.

Elders and mission committee members have not always exhibited proper care for the missionaries or the Christians and seekers they serve. Abruptly cutting off a missionary's support for whatever reason confuses and shocks those in foreign lands. Too often, we in the States operate more like a business than a church. True, we must spend the Lord's money wisely. But is it wise to damage the very work we have been supporting by not exhibiting adequate care when terminating a missionary's support? New buildings and building maintenance may be the biggest dangers to missionaries, as many churches cut mission work when extra funds are needed. We can always borrow money to build buildings, but few borrow to keep a mission work in place.

In churches of Christ, many parents direct their children's education toward professional and high paying secular positions. We don't emphasize a sense of duty toward evangelism. We don't emphasize the personal rewards of living a life dedicated to preaching the Word. We don't emphasize the importance of saving others. In not emphasizing the important aspects of Christianity, we may be denying our children the happiest and most productive life they could experience. I am the first to admit that I don't know how to reverse this trend, and my children are too old to retrain. It must come from parents, bible teachers, ministers, and elders all working together as a team. Did you note in the various accounts how many had to leave our country before they noticed just how materialistic we are? We are like the proverbial frog sitting in a pot of heating water, except we are immersed in materialism and don't realize how much it is affecting our goals and lives.

Some churches of Christ neither encourage missionary attitudes nor inform the youth about the excitement of dedicating one's life to saving souls. Why don't we encourage missionaries to come and speak even though we think we may not have any money to give them? Their adventures for Christ may penetrate a young heart. But if we do that, we must be prepared for our children and grandchildren to choose mission work. How many missionaries return home or fail to go in the first place because their families object? What are our priorities?

Churches of Christ have sent missionaries into the field with woefully little training. We would be horrified if our military sent our soldiers into battle ill equipped and poorly trained, because we know many would die needless deaths. Yet, we sometimes send our missionaries into battle with the forces of evil without considering the training and support base they will need. How many missionaries do we kill spiritually by not supporting the necessary trainers and training? Missionaries don't need to have doctorate degrees in missions, but they do need to appreciate the challenges they will encounter in foreign countries. And they need an experienced contact with which they can freely communicate. We need to support the trainers and the contacts so that we can maintain healthy and vital mission efforts.

Missionaries and supporters should realize that no one knows how to do mission work. A person may have spent years working in a field and brought many to Christ, but as Robert K. Oglesby pointed out, what made their approach successful may be heavily dependent upon their unique personality and the society in which they worked. Mission work shares some similarities to technical research. Just because one doesn't know the answer shouldn't keep him or her from trying an approach they think may work. If it works, great. If it doesn't, try another. Missionaries must adapt the attitude that there is a way to get the gospel message across and with God's help, they will find it.

Every prospective missionary should carefully examine his or her length of commitment. Is it sufficiently long to achieve the desired result? There are several cases where promising works were begun and then abandoned before a leadership base had been built. Usually, the church collapsed shortly after the missionary left. If a person cannot commit for the ten, fifteen, or twenty years required to produce a well-grounded leadership dedicated to reproducing themselves, he or she must make sure that someone will follow them in the work. Churches should also plan from the beginning to stay the course. A congregation must commit to send support until an effective transition is complete. Effective mission work is both expensive and long term. But good work, terminated too soon, may have disastrous consequences.

Congregations should think through the proposed mission effort. Will they commit to finish the work? How long will it take? What are the signs that the new congregation is functioning adequately so the missionary can safely leave? These are not easy questions and the answers may differ depending upon the location of the work, the size of the team going, and the talents of the individuals on the team. Don't get discouraged because difficulties arise. Satan is adept at throwing up obstacles, especially when the work is going well.

Congregational planning should include local member involvement. Maintaining long-term support is easier when the congregation is excited by the work, and nothing generates excitement more than one's personal involvement or that of a friend. Involvement doesn't always mean going to the mission field. Correspondence courses taught by supporters can be a valuable tool to the missionary. Periodic meaningful newsletters can help keep the congregation feeling close to the work. Regular encouraging correspondence to the missionary can lift hearts on both sides of the pond. Organizing and leading special prayer sessions are meaningful to participants and beneficiaries. There are a host of other home activities that congregations can promote to keep the feeling of missions alive.

Building a strong mission program that includes congregational involvement can benefit the local supporting congregation. One congregation began a work that involved several members in correspondence courses, short-term campaigns, and various other activities. The excitement grew. Some who were unable to go to the mission field began to look at local opportunities. Vibrant local outreaches by excited people who couldn't go to the mission field produced two new congregations consisting of ethnic neighbors who moved into their area. All three congregations share the same facilities.

It has often been said, "There is no one way to do mission work." The New Testament verifies the truth of that statement. We find several approaches described in Acts. However, there is one wrong way. That is not to do anything.

Cline Paden wrote in *Broken by Fruitfulness,* Sunset International Press, Lubbock, Texas, the following thoughts.

I want to share something with you from a book I read the other day. The author said, "I used to think that the worst possible thing that could ever happen to man, either in time, or in eternity, would be to hear God say in the day of days, 'Depart from Me ye worker of iniquity!' But I have thought of something worse than that." You can be assured that when I read that, I read a little further! I wanted to find out what would be worse than hearing God say "Depart from Me. . ." The author further said, "Suppose I hear Him say those words one day, 'Depart from Me ye worker of iniquity' and then I hear Him say, 'But before you go, come here, I want to show you something. You see, I made you, and I am not an experimenter. I made you because I wanted you to do something for me. We could have accomplished it. I want you to see the plan that I had for your life. I want you to see the beautiful things that we could have accomplished if you and I could have just worked together. We could have done all of this." The author of the book said, "I would have gotten a good look at that, and then, I would have been turned away from His presence forever to be totally oblivious to the lake of fire, to be impervious of the outer darkness, the weeping and wailing and gnashing of teeth, all of that would have meant nothing to me. My punishment would have been the sight forever of <u>what might have been</u> if I had just taken God to be my partner.

When we give our life to Christ, there is no limit to what He can accomplish through us.

Jeff Hatcher, in Chapter Eleven, referred to our being the aroma of Christ. Just as the smells from a bakery or cooking food stir our appetites, our attitude and actions should draw seekers to Christ. Let's be careful how we smell while we let our light shine.

Printed in the United States
19279LVS00007B/220-288